REDEEMING RELEVANCE

IN THE BOOK OF LEVITICUS

EXPLORATIONS IN TEXT AND MEANING

REDEEMING RELEVANCE

IN THE BOOK OF LEVITICUS

EXPLORATIONS IN TEXT AND MEANING

RABBI FRANCIS NATAF

URIM PUBLICATIONS
JERUSALEM · NEW YORK

Redeeming Relevance in the Book of Leviticus:
Explorations in Text and Meaning
by Rabbi Francis Nataf

Copyright © 2019 by Francis Nataf

Typeset by Ariel Walden

Printed in Israel
First Edition

ISBN 978-1-60280-334-3

Library of Congress Control Number: 2007321380

Urim Publications,
P.O. Box 52287,
Jerusalem 9152102
Israel

www.UrimPublications.com

In honor of our marriage this past year,
In honor of our very good friends,

Rabbi FRANCIS and DEENA NATAF

whose help with the wedding was so
crucial and comforting

And in memory of both of our fathers,
who were not physically with us that special day

MOSHE TZVI ben DOV BAER HAKOHEN (Morty Mayberg) z"l
CHAIM REUVEN ben YISRAEL (Richard Bloom) z"l

ANDY and AVIVA Bloom

In memory of

Dr. YAAKOV ELMAN *a"h*

Anonymous

In memory of our parents,

ABRAHAM and ESTHER HERSH *z"l*
and MOSHE and RIVKA ZYTELNY *z"l*

RONNY and TOBY HERSH

To the memory of my parents,

MORTON and MARILYN BRADSKI,

who played a special role
in creating so many opportunities for me
and gave me the wisdom to choose from among them.

To the lives I could have chosen but did not
and to the one which I did.

GARY BRADSKI

In memory of my parents

MEYER MENACHEM *z"l*
BERTHA KAISER *a"h*

MICHAEL KAISER

In honor of

RABBI FRANCIS NATAF,

a dear friend and a beloved teacher.

REZA GREEN and MOSHE SILVER

CONTENTS

FOREWORD

With this Book of Leviticus, my final installment in this series on the Five Books of the Torah is complete, and an important part of my work comes to its natural conclusion. What started out as a stand-alone volume based on my many lectures on the book of Genesis slowly but surely morphed into the Redeeming Relevance series on all the books of the Torah.

The culmination of the series serves as an opportunity to reflect on the past and ponder the future. Regarding the past, I am reminded of the famous passage in the Passover Haggadah commonly known as *Dayenu*. Often misunderstood, this liturgical poem expresses the sentiment that even one of the many gifts God bestowed upon us in our exodus from Egypt warrants great appreciation; how much more so all the gifts.

In that spirit, I would have been appreciative even if only one volume had been published; how much more so all five. That the books stand on their own would have been enough; all the more so that it led to a popular weekly *parasha* column hosted by the *Jewish Press* since 2014. I would have been satisfied had the column, as well as my books, been limited to print; all the more so that both the column and my books are now also available online. That the books would be read by a few people in my immediate circles would have given me great satisfaction. But that these volumes have made their way to readers and libraries all over the world, and are continuously being read, discussed, reviewed and quoted in so many different contexts, is a constant source of fulfillment and blessing. About all these things, I am obligated to turn to my Creator and respond with a hearty and gratitude-filled *Dayenu*!

Thinking about the future, the obvious question is what to do next. I have enlisted the help of friends and followers and have gotten answers as diverse as the people I have consulted. At press time, it was still an open question. There are, however, two things that are almost certain.

(1) I will continue to write. I will continue to write popular and scholarly articles, but I will also continue to write books. If there is one thing I have learned in my experience as a writer, it is the importance of books. Sustained development of a significant idea simply cannot be produced in the span of an article. This is particularly critical in my circles. For while contemporary Orthodoxy has produced a wealth of first-rate articles (and collections of articles), the same cannot be said about the quantity of first-rate books.

Toni Morrison once wrote that if there is a book you want to read but it hasn't been written yet, you must be the one to write it. How true this is. But what happens when it is a whole list of books? There is a great deal that I believe needs to be written, and it is clear that I will not be able to write it all. Hence the real question is where to start.

(2) While it is very likely that the next few books I will be writing will be devoted to other areas of interest, I have no plans to leave traditional Tanach studies. I fully expect to continue my various involvements in this fascinating and important field of study, but whether it will continue to be my main area of focus is not yet clear.

Though there is much more to be done, the field certainly looks better than the fairly barren landscape I encountered when I first came to it. New Israeli Tanach writers were then just coming to the fore, their future not yet certain. In English the picture was even bleaker. This situation presented me with a challenge as well as an opportunity. It was also the impetus for the title of the series, *Redeeming Relevance*. Under such a banner, I sought to redeem the search for the Torah's relevance from the flightiness I saw in other quarters. I likewise sought to write a contemporary Torah commentary that exhibited the rigor and seriousness of purpose that the word of God so obviously deserves.

Over the years I was joined by others; so much so that there is no longer any shortage of relevant and intelligent writing about the Tanach. Though each writer is unique (and I would like to believe those who tell me that I am more unique than most!), I have already written much of what I want to say on the subject. Hence if my path ends up taking me away from producing any other major works in Tanach, I am nonetheless reassured that the field is now largely in good hands.

* * *

There are many people I would like to thank for their assistance in the production of this book. As has been pointed out by the rabbis, it is from our students that we learn the most. In the context of writing, this means my readers, especially the ones who have engaged me in conversation. Along with all those who have responded to the oral presentations of the ideas in the book, it is for them, and you, that I am writing.

But while I am writing for my readers, I would be unable to make it accessible to them without the help of a group of loyal and devoted friends who have generously given of their own resources in support of this project. This particular volume was made possible by the help of Andy and Aviva Bloom, Gary and Sonya Bradski, Morris and Julie Dweck, Shmuel and Esther Gluck, Ron and Toby Hersh, Michael and Judy Kaiser, Gidon Rothstein and Elizabeth Holland, Moshe Silver and Reza Green, and Nahum and Sivya Twersky.

I would also like to thank the Urim Publications team and its director Tzvi Mauer for their important role in the *Redeeming Relevance* series. They have been a true partner from the beginning and it is a pleasure and an honor to work with them. In particular, the production of this volume was greatly assisted by Pearl Friedman.

Another important partner in the series has been the David Cardozo Academy and its Dean, my good friend Rabbi Dr. Natan Lopes Cardozo. He has consistently encouraged me in this project, long after our formal association came to an end in 2010. I will always be indebted to him – on that score and many others. Moreover, being given use of the resources of the DCA and its able administrator, Esther Peterman, insured that whatever I needed would be executed smoothly and efficiently.

I am fortunate to have been able once again to enlist the talents of the same artist whose image graced my previous book, *Redeeming Relevance in the Book of Deuteronomy*. That artist is Darius Gilmont and it is a great pleasure to work with him. In this case, I am also greatly indebted to Ariella Verlag of Berlin and its very helpful director, Myriam Halberstam, for permission to use an image originally commissioned for their exclusive use.

A new thank you goes to Sefaria,[1] the massive online Judaica library, which has so graciously sponsored the online edition of *Redeeming Relevance* and made it available to a much larger audience. In particular, I want to thank those involved in the project, Lev Israel and Shmuel Weissman, and its CEO, Daniel Septimus. And though he is no longer at Sefaria, I am also indebted to Ari Elias-Bachrach, who was instrumental in getting the project off the ground. I have been privileged to work with Sefaria on many other projects over the past few years and am grateful for the opportunity to contribute to the important work that is being done there.

Along with everything else for which I am grateful to my wife, Deena, the (sometimes painful) effort that she has so readily invested into editing and improving these books has been a truly priceless gift. Her formidable talents markedly enhance my writing, as they do everything else to which she applies them. I am also grateful to my now-adult children who have shown so much interest and pride in my work. Making it easier for them to read my books is certainly not the least of reasons that I hope one day to see the series translated into Hebrew.

There is at least one other connection between my children and my books. As with one's children, putting books out into the world means watching them find a path of their own. So the same prayer that I have often recited for my own children is ultimately the one that I have for my books: That they should meet their potential. That is, that whoever will benefit from them will access them and find the proper circumstances in which to gain from what is written in these pages. Indeed, may it be His will!

— Francis Nataf
Jerusalem, II Adar 5779
March 2019

---

1   http://www.Sefaria.org.

Ending the *Vayikra* Avoidance Syndrome

A S WE COME to the middle of the Torah, we encounter a book often overlooked. Shorter than the other four books and interrupted in its yearly reading by Purim and Pesach, it often feels like a mere thoroughfare to get from the grand exodus narrative of *Shemot* to the fascinating, real-life leadership struggles of *Bemidbar*.

I occasionally run into individuals who truly appreciate the book of *Vayikra*; but, they are the exceptions who just prove the rule. The truth of this was brought home by a panel discussion I attended whose members were asked to name their favorite books in the Bible. I don't remember all the answers, but I assume they were the obvious ones such as *Bereshit*, *Yona*, *Esther*, and the like. But one choice stuck out – *Vayikra*. In fact, the choice was so surprising that the panelist was immediately stopped and asked to explain!

The Jewish nation people has a rather peculiar relationship with the book of *Vayikra*. On the one hand, almost all serious Jews are aware that many of Judaism's most important laws and ideas are to be found in the Torah's middle book. Rabbi Akiva's famous statement that the crux of the Torah is to be found there, in the phrase, "*Ve'ahavta lere'acha kamocha* (love your neighbor as yourself),"[1] is only the beginning. Many other central doctrines are found near the phrase elevated by Rabbi Akiva, so much so that *parashat Kedoshim*, the section that contains them, could be described as *Vayikra's* – and perhaps the entire Torah's – flagship *parasha*.

1 *Vayikra* 19:18; *Sifra* on *Vayikra* 19:18.

Parashat Kedoshim is the only place in the Torah where one finds concepts such as the commandment to be holy and the prohibitions against taking vengeance, spreading gossip and putting a stumbling block in front of the blind. But the importance of the book is not limited to this *parasha*. Going beyond *Kedoshim*, we find many other seminal discussions of Judaism's bread-and-butter practices: If one wanted to know, for example, about *brit mila*, *kashrut* or the festivals, the book of *Vayikra* would certainly be the place to start.

Yet in spite of the above highlights, the book of *Vayikra* also contains an overwhelming amount of material that the average reader will find less stimulating. Many of its laws are directed to the priestly elite in charge of the Temple service, so much so that the book is also called *Torat Kohanim* (the Teaching of the Priests). Likewise, the laws of ritual purity and impurity enumerated in *Vayikra* also relate primarily to the priests. But it is not only that the bulk of the book is directed to this small subgroup that confounds most readers, it is also the intricacy of its details. As we will discuss in Chapter One regarding sacrifices, the reason for these particularly exacting discussions is often beyond us.

Another problem is *Vayikra*'s almost total lack of stories. The noted American sociologist Robert Bellah once described man as a storytelling animal. This goes beyond the fact that we relate to stories with more enthusiasm and interest than we do to dry facts. It is saying that stories are connected to our very essence. In Bellah's words, "Narrative . . . is the way we understand our lives."[2]

There is no question in my mind that the relative popularity of the Torah's other books has much to do with their narrative content. Three of them, *Bereshit*, *Shemot* and *Bemidbar*, contain many stories. Even *Devarim* has more and longer narrative sections than *Vayikra*. All we find in our book is two micro-stories. The first, the death of Aharon's sons (10:1–7),[3] may be memorable, but it is quite short and with little detail. The second tells of an anonymous

---

2   Robert Bellah, *The Robert Bellah Reader* (Durham, NC: Duke University Press, 2006), 10–11.

3   Granted, the death of Aharon's sons comes at the tail end of the larger narrative of the Tabernacle's inauguration, which comprises another twenty-four verses in the same chapter. However, that part of the story is not so much narrative as merely the transmittal of information that the sacrificial rite was put into effect.

man who curses (24:10–23) and is even more obscure. (In spite of their brevity and lack of detail, we will nevertheless devote a chapter to each of these stories later in this book.)

All of this means that in spite of certain well-known highlights, most people will find *Vayikra* a difficult read. For with remote, intricate details bogging us down on the one hand and no stories to stimulate our imagination on the other, to say that the study of *Vayikra* does not present serious hurdles would be fooling ourselves.

Rabbinic Avoidance Syndrome

It is not only us moderns who find ourselves less than enthusiastic about the book of *Vayikra*. Early in rabbinic history, when the division of *parashiyot* was being established, the rabbis had to decide how to divide the Torah into weekly sections that were to be read in the synagogue. They divided the Torah based on the number of weeks in a leap year (i.e., one *parasha* a week), then had to determine which *parashiyot* would be combined in a non-leap year. We should perhaps not be too surprised that fully half of the six double *parashiyot* in the Torah are found in *Vayikra*![4] And lest we forget, *Vayikra* is the shortest of the five books to begin with. As a result, there are some years in which the entire book is covered in only seven weeks. Compare that with *Bereshit*'s unvarying twelve weeks – meaning that in such a year the latter would get almost twice as much of our attention as *Vayikra*.

While the Talmud gives a reason why there was a preference to double up *parashiot* specifically when we read *Vayikra*,[5] this is not to say there were no

---

4   In Israel. The other three double *parashiyot* are found in the books of *Shemot* (2) and *Bemidbar* (1). There is an additional combination in the Diaspora in *Bemidbar*, adding a seventh pair to the group.

5   See *Megila* 31b, which explains that there is a need to finish *Vayikra* before the holiday of Shavuot, since Shavuot is a type of new year, and it is thus important to have the curses at the end of *Vayikra* be read and finished before the festival. But that only tells us why the majority of the double *parashiyot* need to be in the first three books and not why there seems to be such a preference for *Vayikra*. Granted, there are no double *parashiyot* before the Hebrew month of Adar, when the leap year would be

other considerations alongside. Judging by some of the other *parashiyot* that were combined as well as those that were not, one consideration was almost certainly to maximize the educational potential of the weekly Torah readings. Understanding that the *parashiyot* of *Vayikra* would be less impactful, the rabbis consciously structured the weekly readings to cover this book more quickly than any other.

If the early rabbis initiated the trend of minimizing our exposure to *Vayikra*, most contemporary pulpit rabbis push it even further. Many holidays and observances fall out during this time period, and most pulpit rabbis will grab the opportunity to speak about them instead of the *parashiyot* that intersperse them. Discussions pertaining to Pesach often take the place of some of the early *parashiyot* of *Vayikra*, while *Sefirat haOmer* can cover the later ones. Whatever has not already been eliminated can be mitigated by sermons regarding the contemporary observances of Yom Ha'atzma'ut, Yom HaShoah, and the like. The rabbis who make such choices are not being frivolous. Knowing the difficulty of speaking effectively about *Vayikra*, they see these commemorative days on the Jewish calendar as opportunities to speak more impactfully.

Jewish culture has created a type of vicious cycle around the book of *Vayikra*. Because it is more difficult, we tend to look at it less. But because we look at it less, we also understand it less – which, in turn, keeps it difficult and less appealing. I call this the *Vayikra Avoidance Syndrome*.

My Personal Avoidance Syndrome

I am really no exception to the other rabbis seeking opportunities to avoid speaking about *Vayikra*. In fact, with a series title like *Redeeming **Relevance***, more than one colleague has only half-mischievously asked, "What are you

---

ratified with a second month of Adar. Thus if the Talmud's explanation with regard to Shavuot took place before the Jewish calendar was fixed such that it was only known in Adar whether a year would be a leap year or not, the rabbis might not have had much choice. Nevertheless, the Gemara itself questions the absolute need for the book of *Vayikra* to be finished before Shavuot.

going to do when you get to *Vayikra*?" Perhaps part of the answer was to delay writing about it – to save it for the end of the series, and not to write it where it belongs in the sequence.

My own *Vayikra* Avoidance Syndrome almost prevented me from writing this volume altogether. When discussing the predicament with a friend and fellow writer, she reminded me that I was not under any obligation to write it. The world would certainly survive if I did not write on all five books of the Torah. Moreover, if I did not have much to say about it, what was the point? This was briefly liberating and, admittedly, tempting.

Yet all along, I understood that there was something more at stake than just showing I could do it, and making sure that the series covered all five books of the Torah. More than anything else, the thought that kept me going was that it is specifically with the book of *Vayikra* that the Jewish people need the most help. Even if we choose to largely ignore the *parashiyot* that constitute the book, we will still be reading them in the synagogue every year. Hence I felt a responsibility to my readers to do my part in making this book more accessible, more interesting and ultimately . . . even more relevant. And though I came to this conclusion on my own, several followers made sure I wouldn't forget it. Their impatience for this particular volume to see the light of day embodied for me our need to find new ways of approaching what most people think of as the Torah's most challenging book.

I will be applying to this volume many of the methods and approaches I have employed in my first four books. At the same time, since *Vayikra* is a very different work from what comes both before and after it, I will need to add new methods to my repertoire as well. First and foremost among them will be a serious attempt to comprehend *Vayikra*'s main concepts, especially *kedusha* (holiness) and *kehuna* (priesthood). This will make my explorations a little more abstract and a little less rooted in the text; but given that these concepts are so central and yet rather elusive, there is really no other choice.

Torat Kohanim and the Torah on One Foot

Earlier I referred to *Vayikra* as the Torah's middle book. This was not a casual turn of phrase, nor is its being the middle book a trivial matter. In fact, I believe it is of paramount significance. While we often celebrate beginnings and endings, at least two major Jewish institutions show the spiritual weightiness of the center.

On the spatial level, we see this with the Temple menorah. It is to the menorah's middle light, the *ner ma'aravi*, that the other six flames point – while the *ner ma'aravi* itself points toward the center of the Temple's inner sanctum and God's presence.[6] Its spiritual centrality is further emphasized by the fact that it would miraculously stay lit longer than all the other lights, even though it received the same amount of oil.[7] Moreover, the other six branches of the menorah literally don't have a leg to stand on, for whereas the middle light is an extension of the menorah's base, the others sprout out from the sides of that base. Hence on many levels, all parts of the menorah are dependent on its center.

Temporally, we find a similar idea in the Jewish week. Shabbat might be the last day of the week chronologically, but it is nevertheless its center halachically. For example, if one did not finish his personal reading of the *parasha* on Shabbat or say *havdala* immediately after Shabbat, he can do either until Tuesday afternoon, the chronological middle of the week.[8] From Tuesday night, we are no longer connected to the previous Shabbat but only to the one coming up. In other words, Wednesday, Thursday and Friday "lean" toward the next Shabbat, embracing it on one side, while Sunday, Monday and Tuesday of the following week lean back toward that same Shabbat, embracing it on the other. This mimics the lights of the Temple menorah pointing toward the middle light.

Two towering symbols of spirituality in Judaism then, one spatial and one

---

6 *Mishneh Torah, Hilchot Beit haBechira* 3:8, based on *Menachot* 98b.
7 *Shabbat* 22b.
8 *Shulchan Aruch, Orach Chaim* 285:5 and 299:6, respectively. See also *Bereshit Rabba* 11:8, which tells of all the other days pairing up with each other, whereas Shabbat is paired up with God Himself.

temporal, are focused on their middle. Thus we should not be surprised if the Torah's middle book is actually its most important as well. Accordingly, it would no longer be merely happenstance that Rabbi Akiva found the great principle of the Torah specifically there. But it is not just this one doctrine – which may indeed represent *Vayikra*'s pinnacle – on which the rest of the Torah depends. Nor is it even several doctrines that pull this book above its neighbors. The most important aspect of *Vayikra* is that it gives a strategy for how to accomplish that which the Torah is designed to achieve.

From such a perspective we may understand why a book the rabbis named *Torat Kohanim*, the teaching of the priests, is meant to help all Jews understand the essence of what God expects from them. For the sense that the laws pertaining to priests should have been given only to the priests themselves is what prevents most of us from taking proper interest in this book. But it is perhaps surprisingly these detailed and technical laws which provide the spiritual center that informs the rest of the Torah.

The reason these laws should be of overriding interest to us is that in a very real sense, *all Jews are priests*. We are not the priests to whom the laws of *Vayikra* apply, but we are priests nevertheless. Well before we get to *Vayikra*, the Torah has already summarized the Jewish mission as being "a nation of priests."[9] To know what the Jewish mission is all about we need to know what the Torah means by the term *priest*.[10] And the way to do this is to observe how it is played out by the Kohanim within the Jewish nation itself.

The sons of Aharon and their descendants serve as a model for the entire Jewish people. Once we know what is expected from them, we can have a better idea of what is expected from us. It is not enough merely to study the dry technical details of the laws of the priests; if it were, we would be able only to ape their outward form. Rather, the task is to understand what these laws are trying to accomplish and how they go about doing so. Then we will be able to use them as paradigms for how we should act and structure our lives as Jews.[11]

---

9 *Shemot* 19:6.

10 See the note in Rabbi S. D. Luzzatto's commentary on *Vayikra* 11:1, which develops this comparison further.

11 This is quite similar to Ramban's understanding of the commandment to be holy (*Vayikra* 19:1). According to him, this commandment is never defined. Instead, we

What we have said up to now means that the whole *raison d'être* of the *kehuna* is not for its own sake. Whatever benefits accrue to the Jewish people by having a spiritual elite which performs various functions, they are outweighed by the role of the *kehuna* as a model for how the Jews themselves are to act. The Kohanim show us how the concept of *kehuna* works up close in order that the rest of the Jewish people will understand how and be inspired to adapt the institution to best serve the world as a whole.

If we approach the book of *Vayikra* this way, its contents begin to meld into a greater whole. We should not be surprised to see that the two-part formula from the laws of priests to the nation of priests forms the actual outline of the book: The first half (chapters 1–16) goes over many of the laws of the priests in such a way as to show a spiritual strategy. Once that strategy has been revealed, the second half (chapters 17–27) proceeds to create a new framework for Jewish life based on the priestly model just worked out. Without this outline, much of what we encounter in the book of *Vayikra* is confusing, even confounding. Now its various components can fit together with élan and sophistication.

Separation as Strategy

Although we will elaborate on various aspects of the priestly model throughout the book, it is still worthwhile to briefly describe some of its salient features.

We have mentioned that the Torah mandates that the Jews be a nation of priests, but this is really only half the equation. In the very same commandment is the parallel requirement that the Jews be a holy people. While this couplet, *mamlechet Kohanim vegoy kadosh* (a nation of priests and a holy people), is often used for nice sermonics, it is rarely treated with the weight that the book of *Vayikra* actually puts on it. The strong connection between being a *mamlechet Kohanim* and being a *goy kadosh* is undeniable. If for no other

are told that God is holy. Presumably, if we are to be holy, we need to understand how God functions in this world. This is not to be done with the intention of doing exactly what He does, but rather in order to find parallel practices that help us become more similar to Him with regard to holiness.

reason, the fact that *kehuna* and *kedusha* are the two main themes of *Vayikra* shows that one cannot have the former without the latter. Someone who is to serve as a priest must be seen as holier by the people he wishes to serve. If we use closeness to God as a metaphor for holiness, the entire reason one turns to a priest rather than use his own faculties is because there is less distance between God and the priest than there is between God and that person.

Of course, *kedusha* – that which we have perfunctorily, if inadequately, translated as holiness or sanctity – is a very broad term. It is so broad that it can be applied to all people, at least on a very minimal level. If so, what is the specific holiness demanded of the priest? The Torah does not fully explain that, but it does tell us what the priest must do in order to access it. And outside of the Temple service, the bulk of what he needs to do centers around the practice of separation. Above and beyond the restrictions imposed on all Jews, Kohanim may not – to enumerate just the most important of these separation practices – eat certain things, go certain places or marry certain women. It appears that separation from various human activities helps prepare Kohanim for greater involvement with God. But why?

The fact is that there is really nothing mystical about it: When someone separates from the mainstream, limiting himself to certain activities by proscribing others, he becomes more focused on, and generally more skilled at, the interests he does pursue. And focusing on God could essentially be what the Torah is trying to communicate with the word *kedusha*.

What about *kehuna*? While it cannot exist without *kedusha*, the reverse is not necessarily the case. A person can practice separation, for example, if he lives entirely by himself. In fact, that is a common road taken by people in search of holiness. But it's not the road of the Torah's priest: Whatever spiritual edification he is able to achieve is to be shared with others. For one, Kohanim don't offer sacrifices primarily for themselves, which illustrates that the sacrificial rite assumes that all Jews and not just priests need to offer sacrifices in certain situations and at certain times. Likewise, when priests bless the people, the service is completely outwardly directed; priests bless the rest of the people, not fellow priests.

Hence, while separation can be an end in and of itself, the separation dictated on the priests is not. Otherwise, why limit priestly practices only to priests? Why not make them available to everyone who wants to become holy – like the practices of the *nazir*?[12] The answer is that the priestly rites of holiness are the tools that allow them both to focus on the Temple service and to serve as intermediaries for others unable or unwilling to achieve this focus. And this is why understanding these tools is so critical to our use of the priestly model more generally.

Separation as Brotherly Love

We just saw how the concept of *kehuna* is intimately connected with the concept of *kedusha*. This is true of the actual Kohanim. But it is also true of the entire Jewish nation, which is given the task of being a *mamlechet Kohanim*, a nation of priests. Consequently, the laws in *Vayikra* that are aimed at the entire Jewish people, such as *kashrut*, ritual purity and forbidden sexual relations, parallel the types of separation imposed on the Kohanim. Since – as we have noted – for the Jews to become a *mamlechet Kohanim* they also have to be a *goy kadosh*, the emphasis on separation should come as no surprise.

In line with the priestly model which brings a certain amount of physical and social separation between Kohen and Israelite, many of the laws in the book of *Vayikra* also separate Jew from gentile. And like the first model, separation between Jew and gentile is not an end in itself. Rather, it is a tool with which to acquire spiritual focus. Like the priest, the primary benefit of the Jew's focus is not himself but others – more specifically, mankind as a whole. And its critical corollary is that just as the priest who ignores *Torat Kohanim* cannot fulfill his responsibility toward other Jews, so too, the Jew who ignores *Torat Yisrael* cannot fulfill his responsibility toward the rest of the world.

* * *

This brings us back to the concept of loving one's neighbor (*re'acha*) as oneself. More than one major commentator has understood *re'acha* to be speaking

---

12   While there is some overlap in the laws that pertain to a priest and those that pertain to a *nazir*, there is even more that separates them.

about all of mankind.[13] In light of what we are suggesting, this makes perfect sense. Plugging this understanding into Rabbi Akiva's statement, the great principle of the Torah ends up being nothing less than a call for all Jews to do their utmost to help everyone. This is the center of the Torah; the rest is commentary.[14] And much of that commentary, comprising how the Jew is to accomplish this most effectively, is found in the book of *Vayikra*.

---

13 See, for example, Rabbi S. R. Hirsch and Malbim on *Vayikra* 19:18. One indication that the commandment applies toward all people is that the word *achicha*, your brother, which would clearly mean the Jew, is not used here.

14 I paraphrase Hillel (*Shabbat* 31a), who paraphrased Rabbi Akiva. Not coincidentally, he did so in order that the essence of the Torah would be more readily assimilated by his gentile interlocutor (who would not convert unless he received a satisfactory answer from Hillel).

CHAPTER I

Ownership, Pride and the Sacrificial Conundrum

I F T H E B O O K of *Vayikra* is difficult in general, some themes are especially challenging. Near – or even at – the top of the list is the topic of sacrifices. There are two main obstacles to appreciating the Torah's various discussions on the topic.

The first is that sacrifices have not been offered by Jews for almost two millennia. Even purity and impurity have had some sort of extended continuity through the practices of *family purity* and *netilat yadayim*. By contrast, essentially nothing remains of what is arguably the Torah's most central ritual. This is compounded by the attitude of other cultures – all the more so in the Modern period – that the absence of the sacrificial rite in contemporary Jewish practice is actually a good thing. Nor is this notion exclusively non-Jewish. Many readers will already know that such a position is echoed by no less a Jewish thinker than Rambam.[1] For him, sacrifices were instituted only because the Jews had become overly used to the physical worship of idolatry in Egypt.

Nor was Rambam a lone voice. Though controversial, the idea that sacrifices are a carryover from a more primitive form of worship was welcomed and

---

1   *Guide to the Perplexed* 3:32. This is not to say that Rambam would not agree that were the conditions right to rebuild the Temple it would again have sacrifices. But even if we were to reinstitute animal sacrifices, Rambam would still regard it as an institution that reflects a historical weakness, and not an ideal form of Divine worship.

adopted by many rationalist Jewish thinkers.[2] But even if we do not accept this critique of sacrifices, our lack of experience with the rite (and with the killing of animals in front of us more generally) makes it difficult for us to accept that this ritual, which is so central in the Torah, is significantly missing in our lives.

The second obstacle to appreciating the sacrificial rite is making heads or tails of its various details. Even those most dedicated to the explication of the Torah's commandments draw a blank when it comes to these laws.[3] And while the actual details are meticulously discussed in the Talmud, there is very little discussion about the reasons for the specific processes of, and differences between, the various sacrifices. To give just one example, why are certain animals, such as bulls, offered for one type of sacrifice and different animals, say, sheep, offered for another?

In spite of these and the many other obstacles that create distance for the modern reader, the core ideas behind sacrifices are actually quite rich. We will begin our discussion of the topic by identifying a few of these ideas, and then will make our way to a few of the particulars. When we understand the Jewish sacrificial rite within this more conceptual framework, many of the particulars will take on much greater significance than we originally might have thought.

The Gifts of the First Family

I want to preface my discussion by placing the institution of sacrifice within the more general human institution of giving. On the one hand, this is exactly what makes the practice sound primitive, as how can one give to God? On the other hand, this is also what makes the rite more profound than the disembodied prayer worship to which we are accustomed. On some level, there can be no more meaningful bond than the one created by ceding possession of something of value to someone else. As the expression goes, words – which

2   An interesting variation on the theme is expressed by Seforno on *Shemot* 25:9 and 31:18. He claims that the entire Temple rite was a response to the inability of the Jews to succeed in their attempt to do without some sort of physical worship, as manifested by their building of the golden calf.

3   See *Sefer haChinuch*, mitzva 95 (Building the Temple).

are what we use today to worship God – are cheap. Gifting is a tangible way of showing that the words we say are truly meant.

Of course, as with any other gift, sacrifices can be given from a variety of motivations, some more noble than others. A gift can be a way of saying "thank you" or "I'm sorry," but it can also be a way of currying undeserved favor – what we call a bribe. On the other extreme – and this is what we will assume to be the sacrificial ideal as well – one can give a gift purely out of love for the recipient.[4]

Before we develop this further, let us turn to the Torah's treatment of what it means for humans to try to give to God.

While we don't encounter sacrifices in connection with Adam and Chava in the biblical text, we immediately find their children bringing them. This makes sacrifices one of the very first human institutions, coming before government, city-building and healing – just to a name a few basic human activities. At the same time, the fact that the institution of sacrificing to God could wait until the second generation shows that it is not an *intrinsic* part of the human condition.

But even before there was giving to God, there was giving to man. One of the earliest events that we read about the first two human beings, is Chava giving the forbidden fruit to Adam. Despite her rather unfortunate choice, the simple reading of the text is that hers was a classic act of gifting.[5] This is very different from eating or getting dressed, which are "selfish" behaviors and responses to obvious needs. So where did Chava get the idea of taking something in her possession and ceding it to another? Given that Chava had no one

---

4   The three positive motivations mentioned here are embodied by the Torah's thanksgiving (*toda*), sin (*chatat*) and freewill (*nedava*) offerings.

5   The midrash (*Bereshit Rabba* 19:5) made famous by Rashi on *Bereshit* 3:6 suggests that Chava's interest was not in the giving but rather in bringing Adam down once she had fallen. This and all other *midrashim* discussing Chava's motivation notwithstanding, the simple reading of the verses tell us otherwise. Granted, Chava began with the understanding that she should not eat from the tree, but it would appear that the serpent and the appearance of the fruit eventually convinced her it was actually a good thing to partake from it. The first realization that she might have been wrong about this (3:7) does not occur until *after* she gives the fruit to Adam (3:6).

from whom to learn this behavior, how did she know God would not think of it as theft and Adam not think of it as invading his private space?

We see from here that giving to others may have been part of a basic consciousness that came with Chava's very humanity.[6] Moreover, Adam's natural – and under the circumstances, surprising[7] – agreement shows to what extent it was clear to him as well that gifting was an entirely appropriate activity. So although the Torah does not seem to view giving to God (i.e., sacrifice) as an automatic human response, it may well see the desire to give to other humans as such.

Along with the first couple's awareness of the appropriateness of giving was almost certainly a realization that their bond was enhanced by the act – even as the actual contents of the gift ended up being so catastrophic. Chava had experienced something good. Rather than keeping it to herself, she showed her love for her husband by *sacrificing* her own consumption of the fruit to allow him to eat it instead.[8] It is part of our own common experience that putting someone else first in this way is a unique and powerful conduit through which we build a relationship. I would go so far as to say it brings about a mixing of identities that, on some level, blends the giver and the recipient into one.

It took another generation, however, to apply that paradigm of giving in order to enhance a relationship, to the relationship between man and God. A

---

6   One could say Chava's need to give was part of the physiologically based female drive to nurture, and claim that whereas it was intrinsic to her, it was for Adam a learned behavior (from her). However, as we will immediately mention, Adam's immediate acceptance of the fruit indicates that the concept of giving existed within him even before he might have learned it from his wife. Thus, I would prefer to think that giving was part of both Adam and Chava's makeup, as being created in the image of God; especially given that one of the primary – perhaps *the* primary – activity of God is to give. Hence Chava's giving to Adam might be the first example of *imatatio Dei*, man emulating God. See Francis Nataf, *Redeeming Relevance in the Book of Deuteronomy* (Jerusalem: Urim Publications, 2016), Chapter 7.
7   Regarding Adam's surprising lack of resistance, see *Bereshit Rabba* 19:5.
8   Chava's giving of the fruit to Adam can easily be read as having transpired within a context of complete scarcity. The Torah speaks about "the tree's fruit," which is just as likely referring to a singular piece of fruit as to one of many individual fruits waiting to be picked. According to this understanding, there would have been no way to replace that which Chava had just given away.

single generation is actually very quick, given the major – and far from obvious – jump required to move the paradigm over to its new context. Yet assuming that jump could be made, there would seem to be no question about its desirability. For if we established gifting as a unique and powerful way to build a relationship, would we not want to use it in our ultimately most important relationship? Perhaps its obvious desirability is why it evolved so relatively quickly.

Still, there is good reason that Adam and Chava were not able to make the leap. To the extent that the biblical characters understood God's basic nature, giving to Him would require a disconnect between the practical basis for giving and its interpersonal impact. What I mean is that a gift has two major functions: a practical function of providing someone with something they do not have but would be able to use and enjoy, and a more emotional function of engendering love and appreciation of the recipient for the giver (and of the giver for the recipient[9]). In the human realm, the latter component is generally predicated on the first. That is to say the resultant appreciation for a gift will generally be proportionate to the enjoyment the recipient derives from it. Consequently, the concept of giving to a God Who does not lack anything, requires the imagination to disconnect the emotive impact of the gift from its practical function. It would seem that the first human being to bring a sacrifice, Kayin, had just such an imagination.

Kayin's pioneering endeavor failed (*Bereshit* 4:3), and God did not accept it. It is curiously only his brother's copycat sacrifice that met with God's favor (vv. 4–5). Yet the textual clues as to why are easy to find. For one, Kayin's sacrifice is nondescript; Hevel's is explicitly described as being from the firstborn sheep and from their fats (or from "the fat ones"). This clearly indicates that Hevel gave more select products to God than did his older brother.[10]

On the other hand, there is a great deal of logic to Kayin's omission of such niceties: Since God does not need products of any type, should it not literally be the thought that counts? If so, Kayin's offering seems to show a much better understanding of God than his brother's offering. For what did Hevel hope to

9 See R. Eliyahu Dessler, *Michtav Me'Eliyahu* i, *Kuntras HaChesed*.
10 *Bereshit Rabba* 22:5.

accomplish by giving God something better, when better or worse ostensibly pertains only to how much benefit will accrue to the recipient? Would not both the standard offering of Kayin and the more deluxe offering of Hevel be equally immaterial to God?

The quality of a gift to God is actually not immaterial, because the whole notion of giving to God is metaphoric; it is predicated on acting as if God were a person, while knowing that He is not. Once that metaphor is in place, all the major aspects of it have to be in place as well. One very important aspect of the metaphor is how we choose the gifts we give to others. We all know this is at least as essential a part of gifting as the actual transfer of ownership. It certainly requires more thought, and usually more time. This is because the quality of a gift is understood as a reflection of the recipient's importance in the eyes of the giver as well as the level of the relationship. As many of us have undoubtedly found out the hard way, choosing incorrectly can turn gift-giving into something that not only does not enhance the relationship, it actually sets it back.

How do we adapt this to the realm of giving to God? Obviously, nothing will be able to match the importance of God or the level of connection we seek with Him. Still, what we choose to give Him must reflect – at least on some minimal (read: human) level – God's importance as well as the importance we place on our relationship with Him. As we associate a gift's value with the level of connection when it comes to interpersonal gifts, offering God something of quality provides the correct metaphoric associations; ignoring quality makes it more difficult to relate to God in an appropriate manner.

Kayin's own offering might have been rejected, but he opened the way for Hevel to show that God would welcome gifts from man. Once the first hurdles were overcome, the lessons of both Kayin and Hevel were learned and imitated by those who came after them. Noach, for instance, immediately knows to bring offerings in the wake of surviving the Flood. Although the rabbis understand that the larger number of pure animals God commands Noach to bring into the Ark indicates He wanted some animals to be sacrificed, Noach receives no explicit command. And yet he gives from all of the pure species with alacrity (*Bereshit* 8:20), bringing down Divine favor (v. 21).

There is another noteworthy point here: The actual sacrifice of a major source of food in a world recovering from the Flood cannot be easily overlooked. Noach's sacrifice shows a very real appreciation of the need to use that source to communicate with God in a way that goes beyond words.

Similar to those of Hevel and Kayin, Noach's sacrifices seem to be saved for special occasions. The same is true with the forefathers, who also brought sacrifices only in response to a command or as a reaction to an auspicious event. Why they are not given more regularly is not completely clear. Perhaps it indicates that the metaphoric nature of an offering continued to present difficulties long after Kayin. For while a man may be happy to go through the motions and be sincerely motivated to develop his relationship with God, it will forever remain difficult to act as if God actually needs our gifts. Yet without playing through the metaphor – as we saw from Kayin – it is difficult for the offering to fulfill what should be its aims. Consequently, the enlightened man is caught in a catch-22 situation, wherein he needs to act as if God is human while simultaneously knowing that He is not.[11]

Whatever the reason for the rare use of sacrifices by biblical figures, the concept of giving to God at least in theory is firmly established in the Torah's early narratives. No doubt there is still room for debate: what are the ideal parameters of bringing offerings to God, meaning what should be offered, when, and by whom? What is the relationship between the new frequency of sacrifices demanded once the Jews are given the Torah and the Israelites' penchant for physical worship which they had become accustomed to by exposure to the sacrificial cult of Egypt?[12] And are animals the best thing to sacrifice?

All the questions notwithstanding, the bottom line is that the book of *Bereshit* leaves us convinced of the Torah's positive outlook on the practice of offering sacrifices to God. Given our understanding of gifting, this should make perfect sense. Barring a messianic and utopian state where our relationship with God is already idealized and giving to Him therefore superfluous, sacrifices represent a significant way to enhance this essential relationship.

---

11 See note 14 for a different explanation of what was holding man back from sacrificing more regularly.

12 See above, p. 25.

From Event to Practice

If Kayin's jump from the idea of gifting to man to the idea of gifting to God was a major step, no less a step was the Torah's move of taking it from an event and turning it into a practice. Returning to our metaphor of human giving, there are likewise two major categories of interpersonal gifts. The first, with which we are all well-acquainted, is event-based, and is what we usually associate with gifts – presents given on birthdays, weddings and holidays. But there is another type of gift that is even more common, though often overlooked. That is the daily giving within more intimate circles, such as one finds between spouses or between parents and their children. While these circles exchange event-based gifts as well, it is the daily giving that has far greater impact on the relationships. This is because this category of gifting is not merely a show of love; it also bespeaks a maximal commitment to the needs and concerns of the recipient. And that is why it is reserved for only the closest of relationships.

This idea is expressed by R. Shimon Ben Pazi when he presents the verse commanding the *tamid* offering (the daily sacrifice brought once in the morning and once in the afternoon)[13] as the most fundamental verse in the Torah.[14] His curious assertion is not only unexpected in the context of the more famous and glamorous statements in the Torah, it is surprising with regard to the sacrifices themselves. These two daily sacrifices are the simplest of the communal animal sacrifices. If we want to celebrate sacrifices, should we not pick one of the more bountiful holiday offerings? Ben Pazi's point is that even in the realm of sacrifices, to put it colloquially, "slow and steady wins the race." Just as the constancy of daily interpersonal giving creates stronger relationships between people, so too can it create a stronger relationship between man and God.

If Kayin was able to intuit the concept of offering large, event-based gifts

---

13 *Bemidbar* 28:4.

14 Ben Pazi's statement is found in an unidentified midrash in the introduction to R. Ya'akov ibn Chaviv's *Ein Ya'akov*. One could add that instituting the daily sacrifice after the Jews become God's intimates at Mount Sinai makes sense because constant, small gifting is appropriate only in such a situation of intimacy. Up until then, it would have been overly presumptuous as well as an affront to the human metaphor involved here, similar to Kayin's affront discussed above.

to God, it required God Himself to introduce the idea that small, regular gifts could also be applied to the man-God relationship – which Ben Pazi but highlights many centuries after it was indicated in the Torah. The two daily sacrifices which took a certain pride of place in Jewish practice were small, regular gifts that man gave to God. They provided the model for all the other sacrifices offered regularly throughout the year, as well as for those brought in response to many more general situations and individual events. The daily sacrifices took what had previously been an occasional ceremony in the book of *Bereshit* and turned it into a regular practice throughout the rest of the Bible and for many centuries to come.

Moreover, with the giving of the Torah on Mount Sinai, the notion of giving to God became institutionalized. While we cannot totally discard the possibility that both the institutionalization and the ritualization of sacrifices reflect a sort of plan B, there is no question that sacrifices would continue to play a positive role in developing and sustaining the relationship between man and God, as they had for the generations that lived before the Torah was given.[15] Once this concept was in place, the Torah didn't just give general principles with regard to sacrifices. Rather, it set out very particular rules about what should be offered, when, and by whom. Moreover, it choreographed entire ceremonies around the sacrificial rite. The result is a blueprint for how to maximize the effectiveness of gifting to God.

I will not pretend that this background opens up our understanding of all – or even most – of the details in the Torah's blueprint concerning sacrifices, but I think it is a good first step. Let us now look at the details of just one law: the prohibition against offering *chametz* on the altar, as a model for explaining many of the other sacrificial laws as well. Here too, we will need some background before we can get to the law itself.

---

15   Indeed, the existence of these pre-Sinaitic sacrifices is cited by Ramban in his commentary on *Vayikra* 1:9 as a proof against Rambam's more negative understanding of sacrifices mentioned at the beginning of this chapter.

Giving what You Don't Have

So far we have discussed the difficulty of giving God what He doesn't need, but there is actually an even more fundamental problem: on a very real level, there is really nothing we are *entitled* to give. In order to give something, one must first own it. Otherwise, it is an act of theft.

While we often speak of human ownership of property and objects, we all ultimately know that it is really more of a legal fiction and social convention than anything else. In order to provide orderly interaction among people and avoid constant fighting, there is a need for some rules pertaining to who is entitled to any given item and who is not. We call this property rights. But the fact that I have a conventional right to something does not truly mean that it is mine. Karl Marx – among others – famously tried to address this by suggesting a different way to look at the connection between people and objects. He claimed that we invest value on that upon which we expend our labor – the so-called labor theory of value. But this is no less artificial than the traditional concept of ownership. In what way does the fact that I spend my time and effort on something affect the object's essence? My reaping cotton to get it to the marketplace has no impact on the product whatsoever. And even if I make a table out of wood, all I have done is reshape that which previously existed without me.

Granted, we read in *Tehillim* (115:16) that God "gave the earth to man." However, we would be fooling ourselves if we understood that man was given anything more than stewardship. It has been said that in light of where we end up after we die, the earth really owns us more than we own it! Indeed, one of the things that has always bothered man is that he can only give to God from that which is already His.[16]

The positive side of this conundrum is that it reflects a keen awareness of where man stands as well as an ambition to give God a truly proper gift. And so man is always – at least, latently – searching to give something that he can really call his own.

Is there anything, then, that we can truly call our own? On an essential

16 See *Avot* 3:7.

level, the only thing would be something we actually create. But has God not created everything already? Is anything that we fashion, as mentioned above in the example of the table, not just a rearrangement of things already created by God? Yes; and no. The Talmud points out that there is something that we literally create, and that is other people. True, parents could not create a child without God. But the distinct use of their own bodies, genes and DNA in the creation of a new being represents a process wherein the parents imitate the Divine act of taking of Himself to bring about a new being.[17] Consequently, the rabbis suggest a certain correspondence between God and one's parents in their status vis-à-vis the child, which has important practical ramifications.[18]

This leads us to the very chilling conclusion that the only thing that would be a meaningful sacrifice is something we dare not ponder. If just about all moderns have problems with animal sacrifice, there would likely be wall-to-wall unanimity when it comes to human sacrifice. I think it would be fair to say that Judaism takes pride in having had a role in the process that led to this antagonistic attitude toward such a ritual. For one, the Torah appears to describe it as something God hates,[19] a hatred which is formalized by the pro-hibition against sacrificing children to Molech. Since all idolatry is forbidden, why would the Torah single out this particular idolatrous practice unless it was to reject it above and beyond its idolatrous intention?[20] And that because

---

17 The fact that this also occurs in the animal and plant worlds does not take away from its significance with regard to human beings, although it does lead to an interesting discussion of why this capability was given to nonhumans.

18 *Kiddushin* 30b.

19 *Devarim* 12:31.

20 *Vayikra* 18:21; 20:1–5. Here we follow the approach of Abarbanel on *Vayikra* 20, who also attributes human sacrifice being singled out – even though it is already forbid-den as idolatry – to its particularly onerous character. We favor this approach as it is closest to both the simple meaning of the verses and the various other passages in Tanach that relate to human sacrifice explicitly or implicitly. There are many other approaches, and the rabbis in the Talmud (*Sanhedrin* 64) are divided about whether we are even dealing with idolatry altogether here. The opinion that human sacrifice is not idolatry could serve as an alternative answer to our question as to why the Torah needs to mention it, and would thus undermine our answer. Likewise, there are some approaches that suggest that children are not actually killed in the Molech ritual.

human life is so sacred God does not want us to offer people to Him the way we might offer animals.

Despite this, human sacrifice has not only been pondered, it has been carried out as well. Given what we have said until now, we are in a better position to understand why. Moreover, its theoretical value is something of which the Torah is actually quite cognizant. For instance, although God's opposition to the practice of human sacrifice emerges by the end of the story of the binding of Yitzchak, His initial request of Avraham also indicates that there is something uniquely powerful about it.[21] Even if the actual sacrifice of Yitzchak was meant to be aborted, its very suggestion points to its intrinsic value, which apparently could not have been found through a less objectionable demand.[22]

There is a whole other dimension of child sacrifice beyond the question of the parents' ownership of the child based on their having created him, and that is the fact that regardless of the act's theoretical value, there is no greater sacrifice that a parent can make than that of their own child. To the extent that value can be based on the attachment a person has to something, there is great significance in giving something of far more value than anything else we can give.

Yet it goes even further than that. One of the things that makes the binding of Yitzchak so poignant is that a child is something that a parent would normally not give up at any price. Their child's life is at least as dear to them as their own, and frequently even more so. It can be argued that our having created our children and the love we feel for them are ultimately two sides of the same coin. For why are we so emotionally attached to our children? Is one of the central reasons not because our children are our unique creations?

---

21 See Dessler, *Michtav Me'Eliyahu* 2, pp. 194–199, for a particularly insightful approach. It also bears noting that human sacrifice did not always involve parents sacrificing their children.

22 There is another source in Tanach that might point to the Jewish tradition's appreciation of the value of child sacrifice, even as it ultimately reviles it. In *II Melachim* 3:27, we read that King Misha of Moav was able to defeat the Israelites by sacrificing his firstborn son (some say it was the king of Edom's son). Though many commentators are understandably troubled by this, several rabbinic sources view it as an act of powerful (if obviously not uninterested) dedication. See *Sanhedrin* 39b; *Tanchuma*, *Ki Tissa* 5.

Regardless of the theoretical value of child sacrifice, however, the Torah makes clear that it is not an option. So we are back to square one. But there may be something else, a little less dramatic, that we can also call our own.

Dr. Frankenstein's *Chametz*

If there is no true parallel to our essential creation of our children, there are things that bear the stamp of our unique impact upon them nevertheless. For example, reconfiguring an object in a way that would never normally occur in the natural world can also be described as creation. Taken to its theoretical limit, this is the story of Dr. Frankenstein's monster, but one need not go to that disturbing extreme to find examples.

When man elicits a chemical reaction in substances that would not otherwise experience them, he is coming very close to creating something of his own. The most widespread and ancient example of this is leavened bread. The actual science here is secondary. What is important is that when dough is leavened, it takes on a new, airy property. While man does not create a new life when he does this, leavening goes well beyond merely changing the substance; it adds movement to it. The dough literally rises. Left long enough, the process can actually be quite dramatic, with the dough expanding to several times its original size. Were one not familiar with what is going on, he might indeed feel the wonder and satisfaction of having taken an inanimate object and given it life.

In light of the above, leavened bread should be the perfect sacrifice: It has most of the advantages of child sacrifice without its devastating downside. But *chametz* is actually one of only two items that are forbidden to be placed on the altar[23] (along with the natural sweetener, *devash*, which is prohibited in the same verse),[24] and it is in fact singled out as the more problematic of the two. How can this be?

---

23 While there are two leavened offerings that are required in the Temple service over the course of the year, neither is permitted on the altar.

24 *Vayikra* 2:11.

I believe the explanation is as follows: Human ownership is not one-dimensional. All else being equal, something we truly own is a much more fitting gift than something we do not own. But all other things are not equal. It is specifically when we can call something our own that our humility is most threatened. Recall the Frankenstein-like feeling we can get by looking at the dough expand, knowing that it is the result of our intentional input. The pride of offering our own creation is of a different nature from the pride of offering something very expensive such as a large animal. With the latter we might feel proud about our ability to amass wealth, but even if we raised that animal ourselves, our relationship with it remains fairly superficial – and bringing it as an offering is not the act of a creator giving its creation.

Not so with *chametz*. With bread in our hands we can approach God almost as an equal. But this is not what the Torah wants. Instead, it demands that we come to God with the fundamental and pervasive awareness expressed by another verse of *Tehillim*: "To God is the earth and everything in it."[25] *Everything* includes us as well. It is only with this humble and accurate awareness of the human condition that we can stand with the right attitude in front of God's altar.

The limitation on *chametz* puts the sacrificial relationship in its proper context. As a result of its prohibition, our bringing a sacrifice to God can be likened only to a child who receives food from his parent and, in his love for the parent, gifts it right back. The act is comic, and for that reason no competent adult would do it. Yet when it comes to God, this is the situation that we must not only accept but even embrace. For while the child eventually becomes independent from the parent, no matter how much a man might rebel he will always remain completely dependent on God. And though there is an obvious rationale for and even a certain nobility to it, giving to God the few things we might somehow call our own ends up being a pitiful display of inauthenticity.

What we see from the above is that instead of allowing us to pretend to be what we are not, the Torah designs sacrifices as a tool to develop the role actually given to us. For acknowledging our dependence upon God, even while we

25 *Tehillim* 24:1.

express our love, is an essential component of the proper relationship between man and God.

Of *Chametz* and *Chametz*

Most of us have an altogether different association with *chametz*, nearly impossible to sideline whenever the word comes up: the monumental concern that has developed around it before and during Pesach. In fact, there is a possible connection between our obsession with *chametz* during Pesach and our discussion.

Though not all commentators agree, it is likely that the prohibitions pertaining to *chametz* on Pesach and the prohibition of *chametz* on the altar are not totally disparate. Netziv is one of the commentators who builds on this axiom. Similar to what we said above, for him *chametz* represents a human machination and an attempt to alter God's creation. There is nothing wrong in and of itself with using what God gave us to improve our lot; indeed, sometimes we are commanded to do so. But apparently this isn't appropriate in all contexts. As Netziv writes, "The closer one comes to God, the more fitting it is to minimize the machinations of man."[26] This is because our involvement in the creation of something tends to distort our true relationship with God. It gives the appearance of human independence, which can all too easily lead to forgetting God – which the Torah so frequently warns us against.

The one who stands before God's presence in the Temple intrinsically understands this, but what about the rest of us? And why is Pesach more deserving of this type of awareness than the other festivals and commemorative days? Moreover, like our query with regard to *chametz* on the altar, the prohibition against *chametz* on Pesach comes with a significant downside. As with any other holiday, eating proper leavened bread, i.e., challa, on Pesach[27] would certainly add to the banquet-like atmosphere that is called for (that matza has

---

26 *Ha'amek Davar, Vayikra* 2:11. See also *Ha'amek Davar, Shemot* 13:3.
27 The first night of Pesach is one of only two holiday meals throughout the entire year that are absolutely mandatory (the other is the first night of Sukkot).

taken a special place in Jewish hearts is only after the fact). Were *chametz* not forbidden during Pesach, there is no question that we would think of matza as a much less festive substitute for what would otherwise be one of the meal's staples.

Netziv responds by saying that Pesach is different, as its very essence is the inculcation of faith. While there is such a component to all of the holidays, there is little doubt that the Exodus from Egypt is *the* central pillar of Jewish faith in God, and Pesach serves as its primary commemoration.[28] According to Netziv's (and my) understanding of *chametz*, using this basic foodstuff on Pesach would only impede the greater idea of the festival. In building our faith in God, what is critical is an understanding of His total power and a healthy awareness of the completely dependent nature of our relationship with Him, and the feeling of human power we have with the creation of *chametz* is clearly antithetical to this. There may be times and places for celebrating the abilities and accomplishments God has granted us, but the festival of faith is not one of them.

Coming Full Circle

We began our discussion with the observation that gifting to God is modeled on gifting to other people. We then noted that adapting such a very human act toward God brings difficulties, and that is why it was attempted only by mankind's second generation. One of the biggest problems we have discovered in the course of our discussion is that man has nothing to give God that God does not already own. To make matters worse, the Torah forbids the sacrifice of two things of which man might claim ownership and thus the things that would make the most sense to consider giving Him – people and leaven. However, we also discovered that these very restrictions are what allow man to develop his sense of humility and know his place in front of God.

Not only is humility in front of God appropriate, it is a key trait in

---

28 See Francis Nataf, *Redeeming Relevance in the Book of Exodus* (Jerusalem: Urim Publications, 2010), Chapter 7, for elaboration of this idea.

interacting with other people and consequently needs to be maintained in interpersonal gifting as well. For along with all the good that even the most sincere gifting does, it automatically comes with a certain hubris. That I have the ability to give you something you would not otherwise have cannot but create a certain amount of pride, even if subconscious. In the best of circumstances, i.e., when the giver is focused on showing love to the recipient, it is a naturally hierarchical situation wherein the giver is coming from a place of superiority – at least within the specific act. Given this inherent problem in human gifting then, it would make sense to not only learn about gifting to God from gifting to man, but also vice versa.

With gifts that people give to each other, the basic functional aspect of providing the recipient with something that benefits them is just as integral as its emotive aspect of relationship-building. Yet given the inherent hubris that comes with it, the functionality of these gifts fall short of the ideal. Sacrifices which are ultimately non-functional gifts, however, can bring the educational process full circle and provide us with a true model for giving to others. That model teaches that ideal gifting is when there is no hubris-laden, functional side to it, but rather it is all emotive. Like most Godly ideals, it may take a long time to implement, but it is certainly one we must develop.

As the world becomes wealthier and, at least on that level, closer to a utopian situation, there will be more and more people who literally have everything. The solution to finding a gift for a member of this ever more populous group is not to find something so new or exotic that you can still delight them. The real solution is to understand that the way God interacts with people will always be what informs us concerning how to engage in our interpersonal relationships. Understanding this in the context of gifting will teach us to give and receive "useless" gifts with great joy, in the same way that God rejoices in our gifts. It will also make us understand that when we give gifts, it is only a physical embodiment of something deeper and much more profound.

Hence, when we explore the world of sacrifices that *is* the book of Leviticus, we will come to a true and internalized appreciation that when it comes to giving, it really is only the thought that counts.

CHAPTER 2

Torat Mamlechet Kohanim:
The Lawbook of the Priestly Nation

The Five Books

Theoretically, we all know that the Torah comprises five books. Yet extremely rare is the reader who has a conscious sense of the integrity of each individual book. Most of us don't give much thought to what makes one book different from the rest. For many, it is merely a question of content and chronology. But a more careful reading shows that there is much more to the Torah's divisions than that. Each book has its own unique character and purpose, which often transcends its content. Despite the fact that each book basically continues from where the last one left off, each also takes us in a new direction, weaving previous themes and approaches into its own new and unique tapestry.

It is my sense that such an awareness is critical to properly understand any of the Torah's five books. Indeed, our studies in *Bemidbar* and *Devarim* already stressed how these books were markedly different from the ones that preceded them.[1] However, nowhere is this awareness as critical as with the book of *Vayikra*. Its core messages are the least obvious, and much of what it is about is hidden beneath its very special style and rhythms. Being insensitive

---

1   See Francis Nataf, *Redeeming Relevance in the Book of Numbers* (Jerusalem: Urim Publications, 2014), Chapter One, especially pp. 21–22; Nataf, *Redeeming Relevance in Deuteronomy*, Introduction.

to *Vayikra*'s uniqueness will leave the reader with a highly incomplete understanding of the book.

One place where the distinction between *Vayikra* and the other books of the Torah makes itself known is the rather complicated transition to it from the book of *Shemot*. A popular technique used in many series' books is for the beginning of a new volume to review some of the information found at the end of the previous one. We encounter this technique earlier at the beginning of *Shemot*, with the repetition of the members of Ya'akov's household.[2] Although we already saw this information in *Bereshit*,[3] it bears repeating so that the reader can better contextualize what he is about to read in this new volume. Thus, it comes as no surprise to find a similar overlap between the end of *Shemot* and the beginning of *Vayikra*.

The inauguration of the priests is the overlapping event between the books of *Shemot* and *Vayikra*. Exactly how to order the sequence of the overlap, however, is not entirely clear. According to Rashi, chapter 8 of *Vayikra* takes place seven days before the Mishkan's inauguration. Chapters 1 through 7 provide background information enumerating what the priests-elect needed to learn in order to begin their service.[4] In other words, before the Torah can continue the story of the Mishkan's inauguration that began in *Shemot*, it has to interrupt the narrative flow to fill us in on related information.

Ramban[5] takes issue with Rashi's chronology and presents a different sequence of events, but his approach is ultimately not so different. Hence even according to him, the Torah presents the transitional information in a choppy way, requiring us to wait all the way until chapter 8 of *Vayikra* before continuing the story we left off at the end of *Shemot*. The explanation for this interruption, that the laws of the sacrifices were first needed in order to inaugurate the Mishkan, makes sense. But it fails to answer why these laws could not have been learned earlier – as were the other laws pertaining to the Mishkan – in *parashiyot Teruma* and *Tetzaveh* at the end of *Shemot*. This becomes an even stronger question since the very laws of the inauguration of the priests

2   *Shemot* 1:1–5.
3   *Bereshit* 46:8–24.
4   Rashi on *Vayikra* 8:2.
5   Ramban on *Vayikra* 8:2.

enumerated in *Vayikra* 8 actually go over much of what has already been told to Moshe in *parashat Tetzaveh*. There, God also taught Moshe about the inauguration of the Mishkan, which would entail bringing many sacrifices, as well as about all the vessels to be used for the sacrifices. Why was it necessary to hold off on the laws of the sacrifices themselves until the beginning of *Vayikra*?

I believe this is such a strong question because of what we wrote at the very beginning of this chapter: we think of the Torah as one long story, when it is most decidedly not. When we realize that *Shemot* and *Vayikra* are two completely different books, we discover that not all the information that fits within the context of *Shemot* will fit within the context of *Vayikra*. This means that the same story can have components that need be mentioned in one book but not in the other. Accordingly, while the Mishkan and its accoutrements – including the priests – all seem to be a part of the world of *Shemot*, the sacrificial rite is clearly not. In the book of *Shemot*, the few sacrifices that we read about are incidental. On the other hand, the Mishkan is a continuation of the Sinai experience at the center of *Shemot*; it is to be the new and permanent locus of revelation and connection with God. Hence, when the plan for the Mishkan is unfurled in *Shemot*, the sacrifices required for it are essentially tangential means to an ends. As such, they need not be mentioned. Not so in *Vayikra*. Unlike *Shemot*, the book known as *Torat Kohanim* is not about revelation. Rather, it is about the daily struggle to raise man above his own physicality; of being "flesh and blood" just like sacrificial animals are described. The sacrifices are thus the symbolic manifestation of what this book is meant to impress upon us with regard to transcending our animal constitution.[6] When we understand this, it becomes obvious that the laws of the sacrifices belong in *Vayikra* regardless of where they would best fit in the broader narrative.

Man's struggle with his own physicality is one of the central themes we encounter repeatedly in *Vayikra*. But the genius of the book is that it is not just a random mix of important ideas. Rather, it is an organized structure within which ideas are presented with great nuance and artistry.

In the introduction, we discussed the outline of that structure: We are first presented with the priestly laws – which includes the laws of the sacrifices just

---

6   See Chapter Three for further elaboration.

mentioned – with a very specific goal in mind. That goal is to create a model, to understand how the Jewish people can function as the priests for mankind. Only after we become acquainted with this model of the Kohanim, who serve as priests for the Jewish people, *Vayikra* moves on to present the more general laws that will actually allow the rest of the Jewish nation to take on a similar role for the rest of the world.[7]

Without the insights we have brought to light, the book of *Vayikra* could easily be seen as divided into two halves that have little to do with each other. Though we now understand this not to be the case, our outline is still yet too general to bring it all together. If the book is to work as a unified whole, we will need to go into some of its specifics and explain how they fit in to the larger scheme. Below we will examine three such details that seem strange at first glance. Yet once they are understood through our framework, it will become apparent that each advances one of the main components necessary for the Jewish people to fulfill their priestly role.

Nameless Heroes and Attention to Detail

Our first foray into the particulars will be the fault line that divides the book of *Vayikra* into two. If we explore *Vayikra* as an organizational unit, we find that the two halves of the book are not separated by a clean break but rather by a more gradual transition offered by *parashat Acharei Mot*.[8]

7   Obviously, this is only a general outline, and it is possible – even likely – that not everything fits in to such a clean and clear-cut linear progression. One major issue, for example, is the return to enumerating laws dealing specifically with the priests in *parashat Emor* (chapters 21–24). In spite of such loose ends, the theory works nicely throughout most of the book of *Vayikra* and provides tremendous explanatory power for many of its most important elements.

It may be useful to remember here that even the best theories are not completed overnight. In any investigation, one frequently finds stubborn data that refuses to fit in to the theory – even as they do not negate its validity. While we could posit explanations for every law that remains more difficult to understand, it is better to leave this for further study rather than to provide hasty answers simply in order to show that our theory is capable of answering every question.

8   *Vayikra* 16:1–18:30.

Though the *parasha* begins with the priestly service on Yom Kippur, treatment of that service includes elements that broaden the scope of discussion to the entire Israelite community. For one, the priest is explicitly commanded to take sacrifices from the *congregation of Israel*.[9] But even more significant is the fact that the priestly rite is accompanied by a general command for all Jews to afflict themselves.[10] The more sensitive reader will notice that while the Israelites were also mentioned in the first half of the book, their role there was more tangential and passive. By contrast, the Israelite community is given a role that is essential in order for the Yom Kippur service to seemingly be effective, even as the high priest remains the focus of the passage.

The next set of commandments[11] is directed at the Israelites and proscribes bringing sacrifices outside the Mishkan. However, the Israelites are specifically told to bring their offerings "to the priest."[12] There is almost certainly a substantive reason for mentioning the priest here, although there seems to be an even greater stylistic reason for it. For whereas the previous transitional section illuminating the Yom Kippur service focuses on the priesthood while giving the Israelites an important mention, here the situation is reversed and the focus is on the Israelites, with the priests getting special mention. After this clearly transitional section, the Torah can now completely turn away from the priests and continue addressing the Israelites with the more general laws of covering blood,[13] with admonitions about the impurity of animal carcasses[14] and with the longer general section about forbidden sexual relations.[15]

The transition between the two parts of *Vayikra* does not only allow the general law section of the book to gradually eclipse the priestly section, it presents an additional facet as to why the priestly section is relevant to the rest of the people. The Torah does this with an unusually stylized flourish, reporting that the laws at the beginning of the transition were given "after the

---

9   16:5.
10   16:31.
11   17:1–12.
12   17:5.
13   17:13–14.
14   17:15–16.
15   18:1–30.

death of Aharon's two sons."[16] This could not merely be a time marker, as there are other, more common ways to give chronological context. The Torah could have said, "In the second week of the standing of the Mishkan," or simply, "After these things." That the Torah does not use such a phrase strikes us as a clear maneuver to recall and emphasize specifically here one of the Torah's most dramatic and difficult events.[17] Before we get to that, however, let us note not just that the event is mentioned, but also *how* it is mentioned.

I have pointed out in my other books that the Tanach describes people in different ways depending on what it wants to emphasize. For example, Miriam is sometimes known as Moshe's sister and sometimes known as Aharon's sister.[18] Likewise, Rivka is described in several different ways, depending on which aspect of her character the Torah wants to bring out.

In light of this, it is notable that Aharon's sons are not mentioned by name in the above passage but rather are presented solely as "Aharon's two sons." That is who they are in this context. But how so? Moreover, were we not to know better, we could understand the verse to mean they are his only sons. (Since we know Aharon had more than two sons, an alternative reading which still requires explanation might be that they are his main sons.) Finally, the seemingly superfluous "two" requires explanation, and hence must have also been meant to provide an added layer of understanding.

It is well known that Aharon was more popular than Moshe.[19] He may have been the most popular man in the nation – he was certainly the most popular senior leader. This is easily understood. He was Moshe's public representative, in charge of speaking to the people. Paradoxically, his failure in the episode of the golden calf might have actually added to his popularity. He found himself as the man on the spot and he tried hard to close the gap between the people's needs and God's demands. There was no easy way out, and

---

16 16:1.

17 My explanation as to why the Torah brings our attention to the death of Aharon's sons here is not the only possible explanation, but what does seem almost incontrovertible is that the Torah is bringing our attention to that episode specifically here and is not just using it as a random time marker.

18 See Nataf, *Redeeming Relevance in Exodus*, 70–71.

19 *Pirkei deRabbi Eliezer* 17.

he showed the people his willingness to take great personal risks to navigate through an untenable situation.[20]

Thus, it is not too difficult to understand the significance of Nadav and Avihu being called Aharon's sons here. Sometimes we care more about a person because of who his parents are than because of him intrinsically. Given Aharon's popularity, the entire people must have experienced the tragedy of the death of his two elder sons on a very personal level. And all the more so if they were his main (certainly his eldest, but perhaps also his most outstanding) sons. And even more, it was not only one son but two who were killed. Understanding how deeply the people must have been affected by this event gives us the reason for mentioning it now, several chapters after it occurred. Apparently, the profound impact the death of Aharon's sons had on the Jewish people sets the stage for *Vayikra*'s transition to an Israelite-centered book, and more specifically for what will emerge as the main purpose of its second half. But in what way?

It is easily noticed that many of the more general laws found in the second half of *Vayikra* resemble those in *Shemot*, especially those in *parashat Mishpatim* (in the book of *Shemot*), which is the Torah's first legal compendium.[21] What distinguishes the laws in *Vayikra* from the laws in *parashat Mishpatim*? A careful read of the latter reveals that they are almost all interpersonal laws. They were needed for the smooth ordering of the new Jewish society, and thus could not wait. They had to be presented as soon as the Torah was given. Granted, it was less urgent to give the rest of the laws (those between man and God) right after the revelation at Sinai. Nevertheless, the default would have been to give all of them at once. Instead, the Torah essentially stops after the list of interpersonal commandments, resuming its enumeration of the general laws only in the second half of *Vayikra*. This time gap requires explanation.

The answer lies in the reason why the Torah prefaces the general laws set out in the book of *Vayikra* by telling us that they came after the death of Aharon's sons. The Torah is saying that this event needed to happen in order

20 See Nataf, *Redeeming Relevance in Exodus*, 78–79.
21 *Shemot* 22:1–23:19.

for the Jews to be ready for the expansion of their legal code. Let us now see how this is the case.

We can easily understand that details matter when it comes to interpersonal relations dealt with by the commandments in *parashat Mishpatim*. For one, interpersonal affairs are essentially zero-sum: There is a finite amount of resources – not the least of which is a person's time – available to us. If I am obligated to give you of my time or property, it will prevent me from using it for others, or for myself. Thus while we may *choose* to give of these resources to others, an orderly society needs to designate exactly what belongs to whom. For example, the attention given to the indemnity that must be paid if one person injures another[22] is very much in line with our intuitive understanding of zero-sum resources. As if I injure someone, it affects not only his earnings, but the community's as well. And since I am at fault, I am the one who needs to absorb the loss. Because the mechanisms of such laws are intuitive, there was no reason to delay them.

When it comes to laws between man and God, however, we are entering into another realm entirely; for while our time remains zero-sum, the claim on the other side is open-ended. Whatever we "do" for God, it will never be enough; no matter how hard we try, it will always be insufficient. Therefore, why should any limits be placed on our performance of the commandments between man and God? As the rabbis say in a different context, "Were it only that a man could pray the whole day."[23] And what is true about quantity should perhaps also be true about quality and variety as well. Why should I be limited to offering only certain sacrifices in certain places at certain times? Why should there be limits of any type in serving God?

These are likely the questions Nadav and Avihu asked themselves when they decided to bring a fire in front of God that He had not commanded.[24] Just because the priests had already been given their instructions does not mean that limits on Divine service were any more intuitive to them than to anyone else. The expectation was that someone would likely stumble in this

22 21:18–19.
23 *Berachot* 21a.
24 *Vayikra* 10:2.

difficult concept. Consequently, in order to permanently impress upon the people that there are limitations even to serving God, a precedent had to be set at the top. The "stumbler" could not be merely "someone." As the rabbis understand the words of consolation given to Aharon, "*Bikrovai ekadesh* – [God] will be sanctified through those closest to [Him]."[25] Who else would be so desirous to do more for God that they would test the limits?

The Torah does not clarify the reason for rules and limits in worshiping God; perhaps it is beyond our understanding. But the story of Nadav and Avihu does make it clear that the limits are there, and that tampering with them is an extremely serious matter. What is most important for us to understand is that the concept of limits to serving God is not just an abstraction. It went from theory to reality with the death of Aharon's two sons, descending on the Israelites like a ton of bricks. For when the most outstanding sons of the most beloved of the Jews failed to pay attention to detail and paid the ultimate price, the rest of the people immediately understood that unlimited worship of God was simply not an option. If it would have worked for anyone, it would certainly have worked for Nadav and Avihu.

The death of Nadav and Avihu taught the Jews that both limits and attention to detail were required to make them a holy people. Hence the only way forward at this time was to hear each and every particular element pertaining to how to serve God. From that point on, with regard to receiving both the commandments between man and God and the remaining interpersonal commandments, the laws would be filtered through the lens of holiness (meaning restriction) – a notion central to both the specific service of the Kohanim and the more general one of the Israelites.

By placing the narrative of the death of Aharon's sons in the middle of the book of *Vayikra*, the Torah is telling us that the laws of the priests and the laws the Jews will now learn are woven of one cloth, and that just as the former require limitations not initially intuitive, so too do the latter. Only when the Jews internalized this would they be ready to embark on their apprenticeship as the nation of priests.

---

25 *Vayikra* 10:3. See also *Vayikra Rabba* 12:2.

The Ten Commandments' New Spin

If the mentioning of Nadav and Avihu's deaths prepares the Israelites to pay attention to the details of God's laws, we must ask whether the placement of these laws here in *Vayikra* and not in *Shemot* affects their content as well. Are the laws that God waited to present to the Jews until they were ready for them, the same as they would have been had they been presented earlier, or are they altered by their new context? I believe the clues can be found in *parashat Kedoshim*, which comes directly after the *parasha* in which the death of Aharon's sons is mentioned.[26]

Starting with the rabbis of the Midrash,[27] many commentators have noted the parallels between *parashat Kedoshim* in the book of *Vayikra* and the Ten Commandments in the book of *Shemot*.[28] Whether one is sympathetic to the comparison or not, two things cannot be denied: 1) There is an unusually dense amount of overlap between the two; yet 2) their order and phrasing are vastly different. Hence, even if we side with the commentaries who feel that all Ten Commandments are to be found in *parashat Kedoshim*, we are still left with the question about their very dissimilar presentations.

Both *parashat Kedoshim* and the Ten Commandments comprise fundamental laws, somehow more crucial to the Jewish faith than laws presented in other sections. In the case of the Ten Commandments, this is quite obvious and needs no elaboration. In the case of *parashat Kedoshim* it is somewhat more subtle, but only when compared with the spectacularity of the Ten Commandments. For it does not take too much analysis to notice the centrality of many of the laws here as well. Furthermore, the location of *parashat Kedoshim* in the middle of the middle book, as well as its public presentation to the entire Jewish people, add to our conviction that something of extra importance is going on here.

Noting the centrality of both pieces only strengthens our original question: If both are similar lists of the most fundamental laws, why are they

26 *Vayikra* 19:1–20:27.
27 *Vayikra Rabba* 25:5. See also Ibn Ezra, Ramban, Chizkuni et al. on *Vayikra* 19:2.
28 *Shemot* 20:2–14.

also so different? Not only is the content different, the way in which the two lists are presented is different as well. With regard to the latter, the Ten Commandments are given by God Himself, in a highly dramatic and even terrifying revelation; while the laws in *parashat Kedoshim* are presented by Moshe in a comparatively routine address.

There is yet another difference between the two sections which may provide us with a key to the radically different presentation of Judaism's central laws in these two sections. That difference is in the phrases that introduce God, and thereby serve to set the tone, in each section. In the Ten Commandments, God is described as the One Who took the Jews out of Egypt;[29] in *parashat Kedoshim* He is simply described as being holy.[30] If we are to follow God because He took us out of Egypt, the Torah's fundamental laws will be understood one way, but if we are to follow Him because He is holy, these same laws (or ones similar to them) will be understood quite differently.

One place this difference is noticeable is with regard to honoring parents. The Talmud[31] imagines a critique of the Ten Commandments given by the nations of the world, which is assuaged only when they get to the fifth commandment – that of honoring one's father and mother. While much can be said about this passage, what is important for our purposes is the assertion that the fifth commandment is so much more impressive for the gentiles than the first four. In other words, had the Ten Commandments been given to the gentiles, they would likely have begun with how to relate properly to parents. How interesting, then, that this is exactly the concept presented first on the list embedded in *parashat Kedoshim*!

In the Introduction to this book, where we explored how to approach the book of *Vayikra*, we pointed out how the laws of the Kohanim vis-à-vis the Israelites create a model for how the Jews are to relate to the gentiles.[32] In light of this, altering the order here in response to gentile sensitivities makes perfect sense. The laws given in *Vayikra* reflect a conception of Israel as a priestly nation assigned the task of being a conduit for God in the world. From such

29 *Shemot* 20:2.
30 *Vayikra* 19:2.
31 *Kiddushin* 31a.
32 Pages 19–23.

a perspective, the same essentials that the Jews received on Mount Sinai had to be packaged differently and, in some cases, refined, redistributed or even replaced (as a fundamental, not as a commandment).

Another example of presenting the essentials differently to the nations is in the Decalogue's presentation of idolatry[33] versus the presentation in *parashat Kedoshim*.[34] In the Ten Commandments, the Jews are told they must not practice idolatry. They may not betray a jealous God Who, having just taken them out of Egypt so dramatically, expects singular loyalty. The prohibition is personal and detailed. Not so in its parallel in *parashat Kedoshim*; there it is modest and matter-of-fact. The law is presented and we move on. Moreover – and in line with the seven Noachide laws – it is not preceded by a commandment to make God our God.[35] No doubt the presentation in *parashat Kedoshim*, in *Vayikra*, would be much more palatable to the polytheistic gentile than the highly demanding and Israelite-specific exhortation in *Shemot*.

In *parashat Kedoshim*, the prohibition against worshiping idols is followed by something that appears to be out of place on this list of fundamental laws: the laws of peace offerings. However, if the list was ordered with a future gentile audience in mind, it makes perfect sense. This is because the prohibition against idolatry alone does not answer the natural human inclination for worship. To simply tell gentiles not to worship idols and leave it at that would not be realistic. Therefore, the prohibition is followed by a straightforward and simple substitute, represented by this relatively undemanding category of sacrifice. In a peace offering, God allows the worshiper to consume most of the meat, as long as it is treated with reverence. Hence the peace offering creates ample room for the exclusive worship of God. In short, the modest treatment of the prohibition of idolatry, followed by the option of peace offerings as an alternative, presents an attractive model to the world at large.

Different contexts and agendas also explain why the fundamentals in *Shemot* are presented with such drama and fanfare, whereas those in *Vayikra* are presented more routinely. In bringing the Jews to the new Divine order

---

33 *Shemot* 20:3–6.
34 *Vayikra* 19:4.
35 *Mishneh Torah, Hilchot Melachim* 9.

that would be *kabbalat haTorah*, there was a need to stress God's authority. The Ten Commandments achieve this by the physical and historical context of their presentation.[36] But in preparing the Jews to be a nation of priests, it was less the authority of God that needed to be stressed but more His *kedusha* – which is best translated here as "inspiring elevation." For such purposes, a more thorough and less emotional presentation would be more to the point. The central laws in *parashat Kedoshim* allow the Jews to emulate the *kedusha* aspect of God. In other words, just like He is inspiringly elevated, so too were the Jews to be inspiringly elevated. And that is the mission of the nation of priests.

The above notwithstanding, the laws set out in *parashat Kedoshim* are still addressed primarily to the Jews. But they are addressed to them with the knowledge that these laws – and even their performance by the Jews – are formulated with a gentile audience in mind. Similarly, the first half of *Vayikra* comprises a set of laws given to the Kohanim with the Israelite audience in mind. This explains why the laws pertaining to priests are in the Torah, not in a special book given only to priests. In both models, the secondary audience is listening to commands that apply to a more elite group in order that the former should create a simplified version of proper behavior for itself. Hence, just as the Torah does not expect the same level of ritual purity from the Israelite as it does from the Kohen, so too, it does not expect the gentile to leave over a corner of his field for the poor. Rather, the gentile is supposed to learn the concept of charity more broadly, and not to take it on like the Israelite – neither in its details nor in its scope.

We have just seen how understanding specific themes and contours in the book of *Vayikra* creates literary room for the repetition of information, but with a very different flavor from the original. Specifically, we saw how the laws enumerated in *parashat Kedoshim* reflect the priestly role carved out for the Jews in their encounters with the world at large. Working with the specifics, however, will not always be this easy.[37]

36 See Nataf, *Redeeming Relevance in Deuteronomy*, 46–54.
37 See footnote 7 above.

Holy Land and the Torah's First Ending

As we move toward the end of *Vayikra* we encounter a more challenging section. Thematically and (seemingly) chronologically as well, the book's last two *parashiyot*[38] appear to belong elsewhere. Moreover, the laws in these sections are given at Mount Sinai, as opposed to the *Ohel Mo'ed*, the Tent of Meeting, where the rest of *Vayikra* seems to have been given. In short, there are enough incongruences here to have piqued the interest of many commentators and thoughtful readers before us.

Both Ibn Ezra and *Bechor Shor* suggest reasons why the laws given at the end of *Vayikra* are indeed related to its central themes. According to Ibn Ezra, the end of *Vayikra* is a continuation of issues so critical to the land's holiness that they cause the Jews to be exiled from it, the latter being a theme already discussed in *Achrei Mot* and *Kedoshim*.[39] *Bechor Shor* takes a different course, pointing out that many of the commandments discussed at the end of *Vayikra* include a special role for the priests, and thus represent a continuation of one of the book's major themes.[40]

I would like to suggest a different solution. We must remember that had the Jews not sinned with the incident of the spies, they would have gone into the land with Moshe as their leader at the end of *parashat Shelach*. Had this been the case, it would follow that all the stories in the second part of *Bemidbar* and presumably all of *Devarim* would not have been needed. Given that the first part of *Bemidbar* essentially comprises preparations for war, which are of a less fundamental nature than laws meant for perpetuity, the end of *Vayikra* would have basically been the end of the Torah.

Let us imagine the end of *Vayikra* as a potential end to the entire Torah (with the first three *parashiyot* of *Bemidbar* serving only as a sort of appendix). Had its contents been the Torah's last religious instructions, where should the book of *Vayikra* have ended? Important here is the question of how its hypothetically final sections would have prepared the Jews for their imminent entry

---

38 *Vayikra* 25:1–27:34.

39 Ibn Ezra on *Vayikra* 25:1.

40 *Bechor Shor* on 25:1. See also Rabbi S. R. Hirsch on 25:1 for a completely different perspective.

into the land?[41] If the book would only have ended in the middle – with the more obviously thematic sections about holiness and priesthood – we would have a problem. For the middle of *Vayikra* only enumerates more general laws such as honoring parents, loving neighbors and those pertaining to the holidays. Most of these apply regardless of whether the Jews are in their special land or not. And since that will not suffice, the book could not have ended there. Rather, as the people of Israel prepare to enter the Land of Israel, it is crucial that the very physical interaction entailed by living on and working the land be infused by the holiness so central to this book.

But holiness of land is far from an obvious idea. Indeed, how is it that rocks and dirt can be holy? Based on the laws we encounter at the end of *Vayikra*, we find that the holiness of land is surprisingly not so different from the holiness of people. To give an example of the latter, sanctification of the Levites is a two-part process. First, they are chosen by God. Once chosen, their mere association with God gives them an essential holiness. But it does not end there. After they are designated, it is the task of the Jewish people to develop that holiness still further. They do this by way of the laws that they observe pertaining to the Levites. First of all, these laws help create an aura of respect that befits holiness. They also provide the Levites with the self-awareness and encouragement to further develop the latent holiness that exists in all of us. In this way, we see how holiness can actually grow. The more it is tended, the more it develops. And the more it develops, the more it accomplishes its goal, which is to promote awareness of God and inspire behavior consonant with that awareness.

So too is it with the Land of Israel; its holiness is not only in its essence, but also in how it is used by its inhabitants. As they came closer to settling the land, the Jews were charged with treating it with the respect that a receptacle of so much Divine intervention demanded, almost as if it were a living object. This was a new way of understanding what a land can mean, and it came with novel practices. For one, the Jews were to refrain from claiming absolute

---

41 Granted, the Torah could have been subsequently rearranged. Nevertheless, keeping this potential ending in the place it would have originally fit in the best – had it not been followed by failures that required the Torah to continue – helps add to our understanding of God's will.

ownership of the land by releasing it on *shemitta*, the sabbatical year. Nor was it enough to merely let the land lay fallow – a practice that may have been used by other cultures of the time and which was certainly used later on. They also had to allow everyone access to the produce grown on what in other years was their land.

Likewise, the Israelites would be taught that the Land of Israel in general cannot be sold. Not coincidentally, this is similar to the Torah's laws about consecrated animals and other sanctified items, which also cannot be sold. For, as mentioned, sanctity begins with a person's or object's association with God, which precludes the possibility of ultimate human ownership of it.

The one major exception to the prohibition against selling real estate in Eretz Yisrael is a house in a walled city. Yet even this exception ends up reinforcing our understanding, for there is an important exception to the exception: one may not permanently sell a house in a walled city that is owned by a Levite. This, of course, makes perfect sense, as here we have a double dose of *kedusha*: of both the "owned" and the "owner."

The laws we have just discussed echo the priestly idea of creating a model of *kedusha* to inspire and to be emulated, but not to be copied. Laws mandated for the Jews in their land in general are not to be practiced by other nations; their lands are not chosen, just like *they* are not chosen. And just as there is no need for everyone to be priests, there is no need for all lands to be priestly. Thus there is no expectation for those dwelling in the lands of the gentiles to invoke the Torah's laws of *shemitta,* or any of the other laws meant specifically for the Jews in their land. Rather, the intention is for the nations of the world to understand that Godliness is found in all parts of God's creation, including the inanimate ground. For the ground's inanimate veneer only camouflages the fact that through it, man is provided with almost all his needs.

Consequently, all people need to step humbly upon their land, and to understand that their claim to ownership is far from absolute. This might translate into refraining from abusing it, as one might an inanimate tool that he throws out when it is broken or used up. It might also translate into a greater generosity toward those who have no land of their own. But however it is manifested, the main point is to develop a greater sensitivity to God's presence, even when one is involved in the inanimate or mundane. It is to this more universal end that the Torah instructs the Jews on how a priestly nation is to treat its land.

The other laws at the end of *Vayikra*, such as the prohibition against charging interest and the evaluation of vows, do not directly relate to the Land of Israel. There is, however, an important, indirect relationship to the land. These laws will contribute to setting up a holy society in the Land of Israel, preventing it from becoming polluted by people not worthy of its holiness.

We now see more clearly that the end of *Vayikra* was designed as a sort of grand finale to what the Torah has already taught with regard to the new society the Jews were to build in their land. Coming at what was originally meant to be the end of the Torah, it connects a novel approach to land with its imminent implementation within a holy society.

* * *

By now it is clear to us that each of the Torah's books is unique. With this in mind, the individual events in each book take on a new flavor. In this chapter, we explored how this works in different sections of *Vayikra*. We started by looking at the uneasy transition from *Shemot* to *Vayikra*, wherein the discussion of sacrifices seem almost unnecessarily postponed until we complete the book of *Shemot*. However, we discovered that sacrifices belong to the themes of corporeality and holiness and therefore need to be discussed specifically in the book of *Vayikra*, which deals with these issues. The uniqueness of *Vayikra* also explained why various general laws that could have been presented in *parashat Mishpatim*, in the book of *Shemot*, were delayed as well. This was because the Jews had not yet realized the importance of detail in ritual. They understood this only after the failed attempt at more spontaneous worship by the sons of Aharon. And this had to take place while Nadav and Avihu were serving in the Mishkan, which for thematic reasons could not be fully inaugurated until the book of *Vayikra*.

We also learned of laws in *Vayikra* which seem like an actual repetition of ones in *Shemot*. In light of this, we analyzed the stylized reformulation of the Ten Commandments in *Vayikra's parashat Kedoshim*, and discovered that the new presentation was due to the newly understood need for the Jewish nation to convey these ideas to the larger gentile audience.

Finally, as we explored the end of the book, we saw how the preparation for entering the Land of Israel described there is uniquely fitted to its larger themes. Throughout the book, *kedusha* is presented as a strategy to communicate what being created in the image of God means. The concept of *keudsha* is expanded from the sanctity of human life to other living beings such as animals. The strategy, however, would have been incomplete without developing how this concept can apply even to that which seems like the least spiritual aspect of our existence: the land itself.

Every disparate issue we discussed in this chapter relates back to the central concept of *mamlechet Kohanim*, the Jewish ideal of being a nation of priests. Accordingly, each subsection relates to one of the major facets of the Jewish people's vocation. Whereas the first section partially addressed the question "How," the second section largely dealt with the question of "Who," or at least, "For whom." In the last section the topic of discussion was neither "How" nor "Who," but rather "What" – or more precisely, "With what." Let us break this down further.

In the first section we see how attention to detail is going to be a prerequisite to the spiritual life of the priest. The emphasis on the story of Aharon's sons is there to make a strong impression that the priestly life all Jews are summoned to take, comes with rules that carefully regulate how one is to go about his duties. In the second section, the review of the Ten Commandments reminds the Jews that the function of the priest is not to serve himself but to serve others. This version of the Ten Commandments is completely reworked with an eye to how they will be most compelling for those the priestly nation will be serving. Finally, the priests must know which laws they will need to perform in order to more effectively serve as the inspirational force reminding others of God's presence on Earth. This is accomplished with a discussion of how Godliness applies even to the lowly ground.

* * *

Looking back at our discussion pertaining to detail, it is not just Nadav and Avihu who had trouble following all the rules. While we know that attention to detail is at the heart of the Jewish experience, this does not make it any easier to abide by it. Whether for practical reasons or for more philosophical ones, following many rules on a constant basis is naturally challenging – especially today when there are so many other demands on our time and attention.

In the context of this chapter, we are presented with not only the grave danger of not following details but what is riding on it. What I mean is that many assume attention to detail is ultimately a question of bettering oneself: If I do it, great; but if not, I've hurt only myself. Besides the obvious fact that hurting ourselves always, at least indirectly, hurts others around us as well, this chapter helped us realize that there is much more at stake.

The Jews have had a completely disproportionate influence on the rest of the world. This is not a given, as there are many currents that push us away from wanting to have an influence on others. Moreover, there are just as many currents that persuade us into thinking that even if we want to have influence on others we cannot succeed.

Moreover, just as a priest can use his influence for the bad by manipulating his duties for his own betterment at the expense of those he is meant to serve,[42] our influence on the world can be used for the bad as well.

What this means is that the priestly nation (along with all of its "priests") has three choices. The first is to do what the Torah intended – to be good priests and continue to impact positively on the world at large. The second is to abandon the calling and let mankind – to its certain detriment – fend for itself. The third possibility, however, is even worse, and that is to misuse the calling and actively pursue man's corruption.

When Nadav and Avihu failed, they failed as priests. That means that more than themselves, it is their constituency, the Jewish people, who lost out. The powerful example these enthusiastically Godly men could have provided for their people was lost forever. Likewise, the Torah, with all its attention to minutiae, gives a blueprint for how the Jews can most effectively use their influence. If the Jews ignore it, the Jews' constituency will be the ones to lose out the most. And in the case of the nation of priests, their constituents are no less than all of mankind.

---

42 The classic biblical example of this is the story of the sons of Eli the high priest (*I Shmuel* 2:12–17).

CHAPTER 3

Flesh and Blood

T HE FIRST PART of the book of *Vayikra* concerns itself a great deal with bodies, often summarized in rabbinic literature by the expression, "flesh and blood." Whether it is in connection with the sacrifices, ritual purity, eating or reproduction, there is inordinate attention given to both human and animal anatomy in the Torah's third book. While the modern reader may have difficulty ascribing any religious significance to such discussions, there is no questioning the central place our body has in our life experience. The truth is that any religion interested in being involved with all facets of human existence must pay attention to it. Indeed, many see Judaism's view of the body as a salient point distinguishing Judaism from most streams of Christianity and Buddhism.

In the context of *Vayikra* and its heavy stress on the notion of *kedusha*, coming to terms with our own physicality is critical. We need to be aware that having an animal body means possessing physical needs that must be met. But we must also be aware of the possibility of transcending it, of *not* fulfilling our bodily needs in the same indiscriminate and primal way of animals. Without coming to terms with our body, our choices are either to artificially deny it – leading to bewilderment or worse when our body asserts its natural needs – or to simply wallow in it.

Acknowledgment of our animal nature comes with the acceptance that we cannot completely control our body – in the sense of denying it food, for example – if we are to live. Nevertheless, the Torah presents us with a strategy by which we can still exert a great deal of control over it. This strategy posits that just as we are constantly reminded of our animal nature in all sorts of ways, so must we find ways to constantly remind ourselves of the need to transcend it. Therefore, while many of the Torah's other laws address us purely as humans and focus on activities and characteristics not shared with animals, there is also a need for a distinct and thorough set of laws that regulate our animal functions. It is these laws which are at the very heart of the book of *Vayikra* that we will discuss in this chapter.

The Animal that Is Not an Animal

The challenge of having an animal body is not just controlling its drives. Another issue is our resemblance to animals. No matter how spiritual we would like to think of ourselves, we cannot help but notice that we have a great deal in common with entities that gratify their appetites whenever moved to do so and seem to lack any spiritual dimension. Our awareness of this resemblance can be partly alleviated with the understanding that existence is essentially a pyramid that builds on itself: All existence is made up of matter, but some material objects are living – and that makes them very different from other material objects. Of those living objects, some are animate, which also differentiates them greatly from those that are not. Finally, of those that move, some have a soul, which likewise creates great distance between them and animate beings such as animals, which lack it.

The pyramid model does not take away from the fact that in spite of our soul, our body functions in the exact same way as that of an animal. As opposed to inanimate objects and plants, animals use movement to pursue their bodily needs. They seek self-preservation by eating and sleeping, and preservation of the species by the act of procreation. That man must do the same creates a certain amount of cognitive dissonance. Even though there is nothing wrong with man's engaging in animal activities designed for his preservation, they serve as constant reminders of what he has in common with these lower creatures.

It's a short distance from discomfort with resembling animals to the demoralizing conclusion that there is no more to man than animal self-preservation.

A stance such as this almost always leads to degradation, in the sense of acting below one's actual station as a human being. With this in mind, the Torah gives us several tools to combat overly identifying ourselves with animals and reinforce our awareness of man's uniqueness.

The Torah emphasizes the difference between animals and humans mainly by limiting the latter in certain animal activities. For example, fulfilling an individual's basic need for food involves saying yes to one type of food and no to another, whereas on an animal level both choices are exactly the same. A hungry animal will eat whatever is edible for it without having to think or choose. The ability to make distinctions between food in a more discriminating way than merely "edible" or "inedible" is one of the central differences between man and animals. As man acts upon this difference and makes choices, he is simultaneously reminded of the difference as well. Moreover, the constant exercise of choice – what makes him uniquely human – bolsters his identity and actually *makes* him more human and less animal.

Notably, the Torah's legislation concerning our animal activity is almost totally limited to activities connected with eating, sexuality and death.[1] The Torah seems to be singling out those areas of our physicality about which we are mostly likely to think of ourselves as being no more than animals. Two of the three – eating and sexuality – are in the realm of overt animal pleasure. In these areas, man is torn between his natural enjoyment of these activities and the shame that comes with the awareness that he shares that enjoyment with the lowly animals.

With regard to death, identification with the animals is explicitly spelled out in the book of *Kohelet*: "The death of this is like the death of that."[2] For when the human soul is removed, all that is left is an animal body. It follows, then, that observing the dead and/or contemplating death can easily make us see ourselves as no different from animals.

It is not difficult to understand why the Torah placed no limits on certain

---

1   With the exception of the illness of *tzara'at*, which it discusses at length, the Torah has surprisingly little to say about physical ailments. Even with *tzara'at*, the Torah's main concern seems to be related to issues of ritual impurity and the disease's spiritual ramifications and not to illness per se.

2   *Kohelet* 3:19.

other activities. For example, we would not expect any legislation about breathing; since it is essentially involuntary, we are generally unaware of it. The animal-like activities included in the Torah's purview of legislation are those we are much more inclined to be aware of.

On the other hand, there are other activities – such as sleeping and waste removal – that are largely willed, and yet almost completely ignored by the Torah. But the issue is not only whether the activity is voluntary or involuntary. It is also the nature and level of the impact created by them. For example, we are cognizant that we share the activity of sleep with animals, but we generally do not give it much thought. With regard to waste removal we feel a natural embarrassment, and thus choose to not identify ourselves with that activity in animals. Thus, we do not need legislation about waste removal in order to raise ourselves above the animals when we perform it.[3]

As we've seen, the Torah does not limit all animal activity but only that which is most likely to undermine our sense of being different from animals. There thus seems to be two conditions for a physical act to have limits placed on it: that we are consciously aware of it and that it brings us significant enjoyment. When these criteria are met, the Torah requires that we limit that activity in order to differentiate ourselves from animals as well as to remind us of that difference.

There is also another albeit easily missed area of legislation that accomplishes this – that of sacrifices. In this context, it is crucial to note, the resemblance between man and animals. But that is not enough. Many commentators see animals – at least, those brought as sin offerings – as a type of replacement for humans, who should be receiving this punishment instead.[4] Another animate living being's life being taken away is impactful specifically because man can identify with it. Other commentators focus on the animal nature of the sin, about which the use of the sacrificial animal is meant to

---

3   The short discussion of sanitation in *Devarim* 23:13–14 is just that. It is a short note that deals with the cleanliness that is expected from an army encampment associated with God.

4   See, most famously, Ramban on *Vayikra* 1:9.

create awareness.[5] Here the resemblance between man and animal elicited is not at the time of the sacrifice but at the time of the sin.

What these two approaches have in common is that animals are chosen specifically because of their similarity to man. However, that is only one side of the coin; there is room to also suggest just the opposite – that sacrificing animals is meant to emphasize the *difference* between animals and people. Specifically, the Torah would never require the slaughter of humans.[6] That it tells us to do so with animals is meant to make us aware, in the most powerful way, of the game-changing difference between living beings with a spiritual makeup and those without.

The Torah's legislation with regard to both the limitations placed on our animal activities and animal sacrifices is not binary. Rather – as in general – the Torah divides activity into three major categories: the proscribed, the permitted and the prescribed. The goal of the first is to separate us from that which is destructive; in our case, that which will bring us to over-identify with our animal body. The second comprises that which is not destructive and therefore acceptable, though no more than that. With the third category the Torah is aiming to create active involvement with a concept.

When the Torah commands positive action toward animals – for example, covering the blood of certain animals after they are slaughtered – it is going further than merely saying it is permissible and not harmful to cover the blood; it is saying that there is something helpful, and therefore desirable, about the subject of the commandment. In this chapter we shall see more examples of this and come to a better understanding of how it works.

Even more important than the tripartite nature of the Torah's commandments is their graded quality. For one, prohibitions are not the same for all; certain people must go beyond what is expected of others. As an example, contact with the dead is a permissible activity for most Jews and all gentiles. For Kohanim, however, it is more limited and generally proscribed. For the high priest, it is almost completely forbidden. Not only is this in line with our understanding of the *kedusha* of the priesthood, it applies to the difference

---

5   *Sefer haChinuch*, mitzva 95 (Building the Temple).
6   See pp. 34–37 in Chapter One.

between man and animals as well: Just as the *kedusha* of the priest is defined by his refraining from doing things that others do, so too, the *kedusha* of a human being is defined by refraining doing things that other animate beings do.

So far, we have seen how the Torah limits various animal activities in order to emphasize man's innate *kedusha*. In the following sections we will explore how this distinction applies to man's body as well. For just as the Torah distinguishes some animal activities from others, it also distinguishes between certain components of man's (animal) body and others.

Flesh

The Torah describes the place of circumcision as the "flesh (*basar*) of the foreskin."[7] As the term "foreskin," *orla*, is used to refer to other, albeit figurative, covers,[8] we might understand the word "flesh" here as merely a clarification of which foreskin is being referred to. However, the nature of what is being described with regard to circumcision leads us to believe that the Torah's main purpose here is more deliberate.

The word "flesh" is used also to explain God's decision to limit to 120 years the length of time He will wait before destroying the world:[9] "Since [man] is also flesh." Man is limited by the physicality inherent in flesh, and hence there is only so much that can be expected of him.[10] When time ultimately runs out

---

7   *Vayikra* 12:3. This is how circumcision is described to Avraham initially as well. See *Bereshit* 16:11, 14.

8   See, for example, *Shemot* 6:12, 30, where Moshe refers to his speech impediment as a covering of his lips, and *Yirmeyahu* 9:25, where the prophet rebukes the Jews for having covered hearts.

9   *Bereshit* 6:3. This is the understanding of most of the classical Jewish commentators. However, others have understood it to be God's announcement of a new, shorter life span. See Rabbi S. D. Luzzato, who attributes this to Josephus "and others," and Ibn Ezra, who also presents it as the opinion of others, although both commentators refute such an understanding. See also Yehuda Kiel, *Da'at Mikra, Bereshit*, vol. 1 (Jerusalem: Mossad Harav Kook, 1991) on 6:3, note 85.

10   The rabbis (*Chullin* 139b) extend this idea by associating this verse (*Bereshit* 6:3) with no less an individual than Moshe, thereby pointing out that even the most

and God decides to destroy mankind with the Flood, the Torah repeats that it is "flesh" he is wiping out.

When men do not go beyond their animal nature it becomes entirely appropriate to describe them as just so much flesh. Consequently, no distinction between men and animals is made when God decrees that "the end of *all flesh* has come before Me,"[11] and again that "I will bring a flood . . . to destroy *all flesh*."[12] Men and animals are grouped together. At this juncture, they have more in common than what separates them; there is little distinction between the rather prosaic death of animals and the otherwise tragic death of humans.

The use of the word flesh with reference to humans is even more loaded, since it is the same one used to refer to animal meat. (There is no distinction between flesh and meat in Hebrew, both being called *basar*.) In fact, when speaking about animal flesh, the Torah is usually referring to what we call meat – meaning food meant for consumption. The Torah thereby seemingly relegates flesh to the status of other foods; ultimately an object. Given that water and salt are actually also types of food, flesh is put into a grouping wherein life is not even a requirement. Indeed, when meat is eaten, it too is no longer alive. Accordingly, man's body, like the bodies of animals, is primarily made up of a substance that is no more than an object.

That man himself is more than an object is obvious to the Torah. But the Torah's task is to make it obvious to man. Therefore, a mechanism was needed by which man would know that his flesh is tangential to his essence. Just as the Torah limited eating because unrestrained eating created too strong of an identification with animals, so too would the Torah want to downplay man's flesh for the very same reason. One way of doing that is with circumcision.

Two major clues illustrate that circumcision is used to downplay the importance of flesh in humans. The first is that the Torah chose to consistently use the word *flesh* regarding circumcision. The second is reflected in the very act of taking that flesh and disposing of it. As we mentioned regarding sacrifices,

---

spiritual man was also ultimately limited by his physicality (and yet was still able to accomplish as much as he did).

11 *Bereshit* 6:13.

12 6:17.

it is only lower-level creatures such as animals that can readily be disposed of.[13] Here too, it is the designation of flesh as animal-like that allows for its disposal. Anything designated as human cannot be so casually destroyed.

Granted, even an animal cannot be destroyed for no reason. But here there is one: When we get rid of something, it shows that we do not need it. Conversely, when we keep something, it is an expression of its importance to us. This is true not only on the physical level. It is true of our relationships with others, of our behavior patterns and of many other components of our lives. There are things that are so important to our identities that we would never think of doing without them. Conversely, the disposal of our flesh as part of the circumcision ritual shows that we do not really need it to be who we are. And even though the foreskin is a very small piece of flesh, its removal is symbolic of the tangential nature of our flesh more generally.

Of course, the specific flesh removed is not random. In the case of circumcision, it reflects the fact that from a physiological point of view, there is no real difference between human and animal reproduction. As mentioned, this is not a problem in and of itself. The problem is that untempered awareness of this identity can lead us to become too much like animals. But there is an additional issue here as well. We pointed out earlier that the commandments that limit our physical pleasure are a type of push-back to the constant, *natural* reminders of our animal bodies. For example, we experience hunger, as do animals, before each meal. The Torah pushes back, reminding us that we are more than animals by mandating that we bless God after we eat.

Yet some reminders are stronger than others. As the sex drive is the strongest reminder of our animal bodies, there was a need for a countervailing reminder to be human in this area as well. That reminder was the highly radical act of removing a part of our flesh.

The strength of the sex drive makes it the area of strongest conflict between our animalistic impulses and Divine legislation.[14] It is for this reason that circumcision was chosen as the overarching reminder about flesh. Still,

13 See p. 65.

14 This is illustrated most directly by the sages who are of the opinion that the real source of the Jews' discontent early on in the desert was the Torah's prohibitions against incest (*Yoma* 75a on *Bemidbar* 11:10).

the main point[15] of the commandment is, very simply, that the essence of a man is not his flesh.

The Torah's teaching concerning flesh is not limited to what we learn from circumcision and the disposal of flesh.[16] Another lesson is the Torah's frowning on the increase of flesh in a variety of situations. For example, *tzara'at*, the only disease with which the Torah truly concerns itself,[17] often involves growths on the body, which are repeatedly referred to as flesh. While there are many other things going on within the context of these intricate laws, nevertheless, excess flesh in the form of growths is generally understood to be a sign of spiritual ill-health.

Even more clear-cut than the case of *tzara'at* is the Torah's stand on "growing fat." While the Torah does not directly connect it with the word *flesh*, the association is implied. For the essence of getting fat is the growth of flesh, which subsumes both muscle and fat. As we might expect by now, the Torah sees this in a negative light. Specifically, the "fattening" of the nation of Israel is viewed as a cause of its downfall.[18] Nor is it a coincidence that the Torah uses the image of expansion of flesh as a metaphoric tool for that which causes a weakening in Jewish observance – in other words, people becoming more animal-like.

Circumcision symbolizes the removal of our flesh, and is the converse of the adding of flesh we see here. Circumcision distinguishes us from our animal bodies, while getting fat allows us to flounder in them. However, abandoning

15 See *Ha'amek Davar* on *Shemot* 4:25, who explains that the circumcision of Moshe's children is similarly tangential to the removal of blood more generally. Here, Netziv's focus is on blood as opposed to flesh, but the idea is essentially the same.

16 While reduction of flesh may be a good thing, its total obliteration, via cremation after death or even mortification during life, is something else. The Torah does not recommend either and indeed, through the prism of Jewish law, forbids the former and generally frowns upon the latter. The point is that one has to live within his animal body. To destroy our physicality completely is counterproductive. We are tied to the physical, and attempting to completely get rid of our animal nature is almost always an exercise in self-deception. This is not the Torah's agenda. On the contrary, it expects us to excel within the physical parameters that we are given.

17 While genital discharge (*ziva*) could also be seen as a type of disease, the Torah's treatment of it makes it seem more properly understood as a type of condition.

18 *Devarim* 32:15. See also *Yirmeyahu* 5:28 and *Nechemia* 9:25–26.

ourselves to overeating is more than that. It is actually a misreading of our animal nature, for being overweight is a uniquely human condition.[19] As with sexual activity, man is in a unique position to engage in far more eating than what is appropriate. On this level, man out-animals the animals, showing himself not only to share animal functions but to go beyond them – thereby becoming the most animal-like creature around. This is why the Torah picks on growing fat as a symbol of spiritual imbalance. For when a man acts like an animal, he is neither animal nor man, but something much worse.

Blood

Flesh is not the only component of our bodies that is of particular interest to the Torah. Man does not share only flesh with animals. Indeed, the commandment of circumcision is given in the book of *Vayikra* in the same section as two other sets of commandments with physiological emphases: those concerning birth and those pertaining to the disease of *tzaraʾat*. As we discussed above, *tzaraʾat* is connected with flesh; birth, however, is more closely associated with blood – the other half of the couplet with which we began.

While we mentioned in passing that the expression "flesh and blood" encapsulates man's physical condition in rabbinic sources, significantly, the combination is not found in biblical sources at all. That is because the Torah – as well as the rest of Tanach – saw a tremendous difference between the two and what they represent. On some level, blood is the exact opposite of flesh. Humans and animals share both, but flesh could be described as what is more natural to animals and, in that sense, what people borrow from them, whereas for similar reasons, blood could conversely be described as what animals borrow from people. We see this from the association of blood with the word *nefesh*,[20] which means life force or soul.[21] Although *nefesh* is used to describe

19 The human ability to manipulate domesticated animals to actually become fat notwithstanding.
20 The clearest expression of this is in *Devarim* 12:23. It is found in several other places, some of which will follow.
21 While commonly translated as "soul," the more exact word for soul is *neshama*,

animals[22] even before it is used to describe humans,[23] it is nevertheless used much more frequently with regard to man. As Rabbi S. R. Hirsch[24] points out, *nefesh* is above the material dimension of a creature, and hence more naturally associated with man.

The connection between blood and *nefesh* is fundamental in the Torah's eyes. Thus, when God first allows Noach and his descendants to kill and consume animals, He gives restrictions pertaining to the animal's *nefesh* – after which its blood is immediately mentioned.[25] As traditionally understood, the Torah is forbidding the consumption of meat from a live animal here. Yet, as many commentators have pointed out, this does not necessitate the mention of blood;[26] it is enough to know that its *nefesh*, its life force, is still in the animal.

One explanation given for the juxtaposition of blood to *nefesh* is that the blood of a living animal is also forbidden,[27] but this is neither the dominant, traditional understanding nor the simple reading of the text. Hence, most commentators suggest that blood is presented as that which defines the life force.[28] It is the blood pulsing through the animal's veins that defines it as having a *nefesh*, and thus as being alive. Notably, the Torah felt the need to make this association clear from the outset. Moreover, the Torah will reiterate it later on, first within the main legislation with regard to blood in *Vayikra*[29] and a second time in *Devarim*'s recitation of the same commandment.[30]

We might ask why blood should be associated with a spiritual concept like life any more than flesh, given that one is no less physical than the other. Perhaps it is because of an aspect of blood not found in flesh, and that is its

---

whereas *nefesh* is more precisely translated as "life force."

22 *Bereshit* 1:20.

23 *Bereshit* 2:7.

24 On *Bereshit* 9:4.

25 *Bereshit* 9:4.

26 See, for example, *Ha'amek Davar* on *Bereshit* 9:4.

27 See *Sanhedrin* 59a, where this position is expressed by R. Chanina ben Gamliel. See also Rashi on *Bereshit* 9:4.

28 See, for example, Ramban on *Bereshit* 9:4.

29 *Vayikra* 17:11.

30 *Devarim* 12:23.

motion. Flesh, like the rest of the body, is propelled to move from one place to another; it rarely moves itself. And when it does – such as with goosebumps – its movement is fairly limited.

Not so blood, which is constantly moving within the body. As such, it is the animus within the animus or, better, the *nefesh* within the *nefesh*. For while it is not completely accurate to say that movement *is* the *nefesh* of a creature, movement seems to be that which indicates that it *has* a *nefesh*. We see this from the fact that the Torah does not ascribe a *nefesh* to plants; even though they are clearly alive, they do not move. Thus, if the movement of animals is what reveals the existence of a *nefesh*, it should follow that the movement of its blood must show something very similar.[31]

While the above may be the most important reason for blood's association with life, it is not the only one. On a simpler level, the most perceivable requirement in the life of an animal is its blood. Indeed, whether an animal is slaughtered by humans, killed by a predatory animal or victim to an accident in the field, the loss of its blood is the most striking feature of its death – blood seeping out of its body is the most graphic evidence of the cessation of life. By contrast, a great deal of flesh must be torn from an animal in order for its life to be destroyed. Moreover, the flesh is visible before its death as well as after. This makes it less obviously associated with an animal's life than with a mere physical mass.[32]

Hence – according to either explanation – to the extent that we make the tangible connection between God-given life and the blood that keeps it going, we need to treat that blood with the respect due to anything we associate with God.

31 Plants do have a variation of blood, and that is their sap. Despite sap's similarities to blood, it also differs greatly. One of the most obvious differences is the rate of speed at which they flow. The flow of blood is quick, while that of sap is so slow as to be difficult to detect by unaided human observation. Given that movement is what we are concerned with here, and that Jewish tradition understands the Torah to relate to basic human perception as opposed to scientific fact, we can comfortably assume that for the Torah, it is only blood that "moves."

32 Though the point is made that inanimate objects would also cease to exist without God (see, for example, *Nefesh haChaim* 3:1), we generally associate actual life more directly with Him.

At this point, we should not be surprised that the Torah's legislation with regard to blood – both animal and human – is in complete contrast to what we saw concerning flesh. While everything we saw with flesh was meant to mitigate man's connection to it, the laws pertaining to blood seem to allow, and perhaps even encourage, the connection.

First and foremost, it is well known that the Torah forbids consumption of blood, even from permitted animals. It is appropriate to ask: Is this because blood is spiritually unfit or disgusting, like the impure animals the Torah categorizes as *shekatzim*,[33] abominations? Or is it because blood belongs in the category of proscribed items that are too rarified and holy for human consumption and therefore fit only for God's altar?[34] Given what we know, it would makes sense for blood to be in the second category. This is made clearer by the fact that even with regard to sacrifices we are allowed to eat, the animal's blood is still reserved for the altar.[35]

The Torah itself indicates that blood's place on the altar is connected to its prohibition.[36] This would seem to indicate that blood is so important that it is reserved for a higher purpose. But even if that were not the case, the Torah's constant rejoinder that the prohibition of consuming blood is because the animal's life is connected to its blood clearly takes it out of the category of

33 *Vayikra* 11:13, 20, 41.

34 See *Bechor Shor* on *Vayikra* 17:11.

35 See *Ha'amek Davar* on *Vayikra* 17:11 and *Devarim* 12:24. Netziv limits this understanding of its rarified status to the blood of the domesticated animals that are actually sprinkled on the altar, but not that of wild animals and birds, the first of which is never brought as an offering and the latter of which is brought infrequently. See Ramban on *Vayikra* 17:11, who deals with this issue in a similar fashion.

One advantage to Netziv's approach, as we will soon see, is that it helps explain the distinction between these three types of creatures when it comes to the commandment of covering the blood. However, it still seems simpler to generalize and say that the blood is of an elevated nature in all animals, and that what is lacking in the case of wild animals and birds is not in the blood, but rather in the animals themselves. To put it another way, all blood is rarified and that is why we do not eat it. Yet some blood is more rarified than others, and that is why the blood of only some animals has a place on the altar. Nevertheless, the fact that it is the *blood* that serves to atone as opposed to another part of the animal speaks to the importance of blood more generally. This appears to be the approach of *Bechor Shor*.

36 *Vayikra* 17:11.

"abominations" and presumably puts it into the second category, that of items sacrosanct.[37] Yet regardless of which category it is put into, blood is clearly not to be treated in the same way as an animal's more lowly flesh.

Moreover, not only does the Torah prohibit the consumption of a kosher animal's blood, it even requires that it be covered after the animal is slaughtered. The most obvious reason for covering the blood is that its elevated status requires us to take extra precautions and make a fence to prevent us from partaking of it.[38] But there could be another, even more positive reason for it: Covering blood with dirt may be modeled on human burial. It is quite possible that we are meant to honor the blood of animals in the same way that we honor the remains of a human being.[39]

Although what we have just explored seems clearly in line with our understanding of the Torah's perspective on blood, it is complicated by the fact that we are not commanded to cover the blood of all kosher animals but rather only that of fowl and those of a wild species. This too need not be a problem, however, as it lends greater support to our suggestion that blood is associated

---

37 See *HaKetav veHaKabbalah* on *Devarim* 12:24, who gives a different reason for its rarified status based on its comparison with water. However, he inexplicably generalizes the idea to all (or at least, some other) forbidden foods, citing the famous statement (*Sifra, Kedoshim* 12:23) that when asked whether we would want to eat pig, we should not answer, "No," but rather, "Yes, but it is forbidden to me." In fact, that statement does not seem to have anything to do with the spiritual desirability of the food but rather its taste.

38 Many commentators note that the animals whose blood we do *not* cover are precisely the ones whose blood goes on the altar (see note 35 above). Since this presumably means that their blood is of an even higher status, would we not be even more concerned about consumption of blood from those animals, being more likely to require covering the blood? But *Bechor Shor* (on *Vayikra* 17:11) explains thus: We are less likely to consume blood that we know goes on the altar, and therefore such blood does not require a fence. Rather, it is the blood that we never see on the altar that we might treat simply as meat. For this reason the Torah gives us an extra reminder here and tells us to cover *that* blood.

39 See *Sefer haChinuch*, mitzva 187 (Covering the Blood), who – while presenting a very different reason – also gives a positive reason for covering blood. Indeed, this commandment is mysterious enough to generate many different explanations, both positive and negative. The reader is particularly encouraged to see those of Rabbi S. R. Hirsch on *Vayikra* 17:13 and of Rambam in *Guide to the Perplexed* 3:46.

with life on account of its own movement within the body. Given that we associate life with movement, the more movement found within an animal, the *more* life we associate with it. Birds and wild animals are certainly more animated than domesticated animals, and although these two groups are not considered more elevated than the domesticated animals – we see just the opposite regarding which are suitable to go on the altar – as far as the life which blood is meant to represent, the blood of these more active animals is somehow *truer* than the blood of the more lethargic, domesticated ones. Hence covering their blood gives greater honor to the blood most representative of life.

So far we have discussed animal blood, but as we found with flesh, the same general associations that we find with animals also exist with people. If anything, the connection between blood and life is even stronger in humans. Hence, a common term in the Torah used to describe the killing of others is "spilling blood," or in shortened form, just "blood." Indeed, the first time the prohibition against murder appears in the Torah, it is described as the spilling of a man's blood.[40] As with an animal, spilling the blood of a man means to take away his life force.

The Torah's approach to spilling the blood of an animal shows that killing animals for food is only barely acceptable; in fact, it was not permitted until after the Flood. Since God is the source of life, man should ideally not be the one to determine when it is emptied out of any creature. When it comes to people, however, the Torah leaves no room for ambiguity – killing is completely unacceptable. In describing killing as the spilling of a man's blood, the Torah is making clear that the killer is trespassing into the realm of that which belongs to God.

An additional example of the special place human blood has in the Torah is with regard to menstruation. This may seem surprising at first. Menstrual blood makes a woman ritually *impure*, and therefore our immediate assumption would be that this particular blood is not only not elevated, but even debased. Such an assumption misses an important nuance: We bury a human body out of respect for it, yet there is nothing more ritually impure than a

40 *Bereshit* 9:5–6.

human corpse. And a corpse's blood – even when outside the body – has the same level of impurity as that of the corpse itself. Revealingly, this is not the case for any of the body's other fluids. Like the body itself, blood is intimately connected with human life. And the connection with life which gives blood greater sanctity while living also brings about greater spiritual impurity when it is no longer alive.

We can conclude from this that blood – even menstrual blood – is far from being *intrinsically* impure. On the contrary, it possesses the highest degree of holiness possible for a physical being. It is precisely for this reason that termination of its life is so dissonant, and it is this dissonance that generates impurity.[41] For menstruation is a small-scale example of death.[42] It is the death of egg cells that could have resulted in a human life. Consequently, the impurity of menstrual blood is not an indication of blood's lowliness. Rather, it shows that when blood "dies," it creates a powerful dissonance that we call impurity.

Blood may ultimately be an animal component of man, but the Torah's associations and laws pertaining to it show blood to be an elevated component nevertheless. Blood is indicative of life and of the Source of life. While man's unique soul and Divine image are obviously even more elevated than his blood, for man to contemplate his life force as represented by his blood is not only noncorrosive, it is actually positive.

---

41 Ritually slaughtered animals and their blood do not generate impurity, however, as they will be used for a more valuable purpose: sacrifices or human nourishment. Accordingly, when an animal dies without ritual slaughter it becomes impure because it will not ever be put to any higher purpose.

42 Among the many contemporary writers who discuss this idea is R. Norman Lamm in *A Hedge of Roses* (New York: Feldheim, 1966), 83–84, who in turn cites R. David Tzvi Hoffmann. The basic idea connecting loss of potential life to impurity can be traced back at least to Rabbi Yehuda haLevi (*Kuzari* 2:60). See also Jacob Milgrom's treatment of this topic in his *Leviticus 1–16* (New York: Doubleday, 1991), 767. I thank R. Elli Fischer for reminding me of the citation in *Kuzari* and R. Gil Student for pointing me to Milgrom.

Humans, Animals and Plants

Flesh and blood are not the only animal components of man to which the Torah relates. However, they are the main ones, and they set up the boundaries between that which we need to distance ourselves from and that which we can embrace – essentially, physical substance on the one hand and animate life on the other.

But before we can conclude our discussion, there is one more point of comparison between man and other living things worth exploring: that which the Torah calls *zera*, or seed. Notably, just as the word for flesh, *basar*, is used when referring to both humans and animals, so too, classical Hebrew uses essentially the same word for the seed of both people and other living beings – in this case plants. Rabbi S. R. Hirsch picks up on this when the noun becomes a verb and is used to describe the conception of a child. He notes, that this usage is quite unusual, as the Torah does not normally employ the root *zayin, reish, ayin* for humans; the word *lehazria*, "seeding," is an expression otherwise reserved for plant reproduction.[43]

Rabbi Hirsch's point about this is actually already conveyed just by the common use of the noun *zera* for plants and humans alike. In either case, the Torah seems to be reminding us that there is ultimately very little difference between the function of human seed and the function of plant seed. For whereas human sexuality resembles animal sexuality and not that of plants, actual conception is essentially the same in all three. It is neither willed nor controllable. Accordingly, conception is described in terms that pertain to plants, the lowest and most passive of the life forms in which it is found. It thus seems that man must confront not only that which he shares with the animals, but that which he shares with plants as well.

Considering human life the equivalent of plant life is potentially even more dangerous than identifying ourselves with animals. The danger would not be overindulgence in creature pleasures, as it would be if we were to "act like animals," but rather listlessness and passivity. Put differently, over-identification with animals may lead us to too much activity, whereas overly identifying with

43 Rabbi S. R. Hirsch, *Vayikra* 12:2.

our vegetal side may lead us to too little. For Rabbi Hirsch, this is characteristically a rejection of human freedom in favor of the totally constrained life of plants. But even without going that far, we can certainly acknowledge the catastrophe that would be wrought by excessive passivity.

While the Torah truly seems to be interested in making this point as well, it puts much greater emphasis on the more common danger of identifying with our animal side. Hence, it is not at all clear whether the Torah's legislation regarding plant seed and human seed emerges from this or from other considerations. For example, the Torah's prohibition against mixing seeds in a field seems to be an extension of the prohibitions against mixing species more generally, not a statute designed to teach people something about themselves. Even the impurity generated by conception – once the process is completed and the child is born – which Rabbi Hirsch sees as evidence for his point,[44] is likely to be more closely connected with the birthing mother's bleeding at childbirth than with anything else. Be that as it may, there is good reason to say the Torah wants us never to think of ourselves as being essentially the same as plants.

Flesh and Blood

Human actions can be divided between those focused on ourselves and those focused on others. The former generally center on our animal bodies, while the latter often connect us with our Divine souls. This is no coincidence: Animals are created to serve themselves, whereas God – having no such need – takes care of others. But this should not lead us to the conclusion that man's animal side is devoid of God. Quite the contrary. In this chapter, we have seen how the Torah maximizes our awareness of God even when we are focused on our animal existence. We saw that this awareness is maximized, more than anything else, by contemplating the nature of blood. For when we think about its

---

44 For R. Hirsch, the impurity is related to the danger of being overly influenced by the involuntary, plant-like nature of conception and pregnancy.

life-giving properties and its constant movement throughout the body, we are easily led to the contemplation of God Himself.

Yet the wonders of blood are only one side of the equation. Much of this chapter was a study in contrasts between blood on the one hand, and flesh on the other. We discovered that in the same way that contemplation of blood can be uplifting, contemplation of flesh can be proportionately degrading. The problem is that these contrasting elements are tightly integrated into one whole, and therefore thinking about blood without also thinking about flesh is no simple feat.

When the rabbis coined (or at least adopted) the phrase "flesh and blood," bringing these two disparate elements together, they might have had precisely this in mind. Rather than telling us to fight the dissonance between flesh and blood, the rabbis encouraged us to consider them together. If thinking of our bodies as both flesh and blood has the distinct disadvantage of reminding us about our flesh, this is more than made up for by the fact that it prevents us from ever seeing our flesh in isolation. As the rabbis thereby grant that a human being cannot be blood without flesh, they are able to make the crucial point that neither is he ever flesh without blood.

Combining flesh with blood can be seen as part of a larger pattern wherein everything in existence is imbued with spiritually redeeming qualities. The great benefit of such an arrangement is that it facilitates our understanding that there can be no place or thing that is devoid of God.

In the case of flesh, simultaneous cognizance of blood helps us remember that what animates every part of our body – and ultimately gives it worth – is its Divine life source. Perhaps it was with this in mind that in the midst of great physical degradation, Iyov could still call out his immortal words, "From my *flesh* will I see God."[45]

---

45 *Iyov* 19:26, according to the interpretation of R. Bachya ibn Pakuda in *Duties of the Heart*, Second Treatise on Examination 5:3.

CHAPTER 4

Youth, Talent and Sin

Aᴌᴌ ʀᴇᴀᴅᴇʀs ᴏғ the Bible know that some stories are narrated at great length, while others are told in a terse sentence or two. In most cases, a story told in detail indicates its importance. This, for example, is the conclusion of the rabbis[1] in response to the detail in the story of Avraham's servant's sojourn to find a wife for Yitzchak.[2]

And what is true of the Torah as a whole is true of particular stories as well. One glaring example is the binding of Yitzchak. Avraham's journey to the place is described excruciatingly slowly over seven verses,[3] while his return consists of only one.[4] As once he has passed the test, his return is almost tangential.

This principle is turned on its head in the story of Aharon's sons, Nadav and Avihu, bringing an unauthorized fire into the newly built Mishkan (*Vayikra* 10). What appears to be the focus is recounted quickly, while the more tangential sections are discussed at length: While the description of Nadav and Avihu's dramatic sin comprises only two verses, the reaction of others – especially that of Aharon – is discussed in great detail in the remaining eighteen verses of the chapter.

In spite of its sparse description, Nadav and Avihu's sin would be exceedingly difficult to consider a mere footnote to Aharon's reaction; the drama

---

1   *Bereshit Rabba* 60:8.
2   *Bereshit* 24:2–66.
3   22:3–9.
4   22:19.

created by its placement right after the inauguration of the Mishkan and the immediate and supernatural death of two of Israel's highest leaders cannot help but make a strong impression. And as discussed in Chapter Two its mention again at a critical juncture later in *Vayikra* emphasizes its significance to those who lived through it as well.[5] We can only conclude that the imbalance of attention given to the events in this story do not seem to be an indication of their relative weight.

It may be helpful to think of the relationship between the two sections of the story as similar to the relationship between a text and its commentary. In the vast majority of cases, a commentary seeking to explain a text will be longer than the text itself. Moreover, the richer the text, the longer the commentary. Here too, the much longer description that follows the actual "main event" will greatly bolster our understanding of the latter.

Before we attempt to analyze this contextualization, however, we must first try to understand what actually happened. The surprising lack of clarity will help us appreciate why this story requires such an elaborate interpretive lens for it to work.

What Was Nadav and Avihu's Sin?

At first glance, Nadav and Avihu's sin seems quite straightforward. The Torah tells us that they "brought in front of God a foreign fire that He did not command."[6] Granted, we do not know the exact details of this fire and in what way it was brought in front of God, nor is it clear exactly why this should have resulted in an immediate and direct death sentence from God. While these issues have understandably led to much discussion and conjecture among the commentators, they do not take away from the fact that the Torah spells out the basic content of the sin. And were it not obvious enough here in *Vayikra*

5   See pp. 46–49.
6   *Vayikra* 10:1.

10, where it actually took place, the Torah retells their sin twice more in various contexts.[7]

Why, then, do so many commentators, even as far back as the rabbis whose discussions comprise the Midrash, still feel a need to search for a sin different from that which seems obvious from the text?

One of the most famous conjectures as to Nadav and Avihu's sin is that they decided the law on their own in front of their teacher, Moshe.[8] Another is that they did not marry.[9] And there are many more conjectures. Other commentaries do not seek to give an alternative sin, but rather to explain what might have led to Nadav and Avihu's bringing an unauthorized fire. An example of this is the suggestion that they brought the fire because they were inebriated (although it is also possible to understand their drunkenness as the sin itself). There is actually strong textual support for this opinion. For one, the prohibition of performing the sacrificial service while inebriated is the first Divine directive given after the event.[10] Even more significant is that the directive is given specifically to Aharon. In the entire book of *Vayikra*, this is the only place where God speaks only to Aharon; even the laws of the priests were generally given to Moshe. Is this not a clear indication of an immediate message that relates to what had just happened to Aharon's two children?[11] Yet – like the charge of the unauthorized fire – many commentators push this aside.

Technical issues might have prevented some rabbis from going along with the possibilities most grounded in the text. For example, if the sin was really

7   *Bemidbar* 3:4, 26:61. See *Vayikra Rabba* 20:8, where some rabbis suggest the Torah reiterates the sin specifically so that readers will not speculate about their having committed other sins!

8   *Sifra, Mechilta Miluim* 2:32.

9   *Vayikra* 20:9.

10   10:8–11.

11   This is pointed out by Rabbi Shimon in *Vayikra Rabba* 12:1 and subsequently endorsed by Rashi on *Vayikra* 10:2. Rabbi S. D. Luzzatto on 10:9 is the only commentator I have seen who takes full stock of the evidence and still denies the contention that Nadav and Avihu performed the sacrificial service while drunk. According to him, God took the opportunity to add an additional angle to the sacrificial protocol while Aharon and his other sons were, ostensibly, carefully reviewing the rest of those *halachot*.

serving in the Mishkan while drunk, how can they be punished before the law had been given?[12] Likewise in the case of the unauthorized fire. Since the Torah states only that this had not been commanded by God, the implication is that bringing an unauthorized fire had also not been expressly forbidden. Consequently, there should be no punishment attached to it.

Nevertheless, a strong argument can also be made that serving while drunk is at the very least imprudent, and that while not everything that isn't specifically commanded is forbidden, this is not the case with regard to the strictly regimented sacrificial ritual. In this very delicate area, it makes sense to assume that everything not clearly permitted is automatically forbidden. Hence one senses that there is another, more fundamental reason that leads to resistance among some commentators to taking the text and its open implications at face value.

It appears that although the meaning of the Torah's words here – that they brought a fire before God that He had not commanded – is clear enough, this does not automatically mean that the literal understanding makes sense. Accordingly, the problem many readers might have with Nadav and Avihu's serving while drunk and offering an unauthorized fire is not that the prohibition against performing the sacrificial service while drunk was not obvious to them, but just the opposite; it was *too* obvious to them.

The reasoning behind such an opinion is the following: Sin generally comes from one of two reasons – not knowing something is forbidden and perceived personal pleasure or benefit. If the sin of Nadav and Avihu is merely that they "brought in front of God a foreign fire that He did not command," neither reason seems relevant. To believe that the sons of Aharon did not know that bringing an unauthorized fire into the Mishkan was prohibited would be a stretch. As for personal pleasure, in what way would Nadav and Avihu get any more pleasure by bringing forbidden fire than by bringing permitted fire? One can always find ways to explain their sin in such a way as to make it align with either of the above reasons, but this would entail compromising on the most straightforward readings of the story.

There is actually another reason people sin, and that is the personal

---

12 See Mizrachi on *Vayikra* 10:1.

deficiencies of the sinner. A person might sin out of stupidity, perversity or any of a host of other negative characteristics and pathologies. For the purpose of our story, this too seems a dead end. For one, Moshe's words to Aharon immediately after his sons were struck – that God had told him that He would be sanctified by those close to Him[13] – seem to be words of consolation. If Moshe was truly praising Aharon's lost children, it only strengthens what is in any case the most likely reading of "those close to Him" – that Nadav and Avihu had been spiritually close to God and hence of a very lofty spiritual stature.[14]

But there is more. Earlier, at Mount Sinai, Moshe was commanded to have an elite group go up the mountain with him. This group consisted of Aharon, the seventy elders, Nadav and Avihu.[15] Here it is important to remember that Aharon had four sons and not just these two, yet they were the only sons invited up the mountain. Despite the fact that one could find other reasons for Elazar and Itamar's exclusion from the roster, Nadav and Avihu would certainly not have been chosen for this honor were they not men of stature.

The above argument eliminates the possibility that Nadav and Avihu's sins were the result of negative character traits. It likewise makes it unlikely that they sinned for personal benefit or pleasure. The only conclusion left is that the sin was something they would not know was wrong. And this seems to be the main conclusion taken by those who reject the simple explanation in the text.

Let us now return to the two examples of this approach mentioned above. First, that they taught the law in front of Moshe, is not so obvious a sin once we think about it. After all, we know that Moshe learned things from others, such

---

13 *Vayikra* 10:3.

14 See, however, Abarbanel, who explains that the closeness referred to here is not spiritual but rather physical. In other words, God told Moshe that there would be "workplace accidents" in the Mishkan. This means that according to Abarbanel, when Moshe mentions Nadav and Avihu's closeness to God, he is describing their vocation and not saying anything about their characters. See also Menachem Bula, *Da'at Mikra, Vayikra*, vol. 1, on 10:4, who also raises such an approach as a possibility, although he integrates it with the more common approach that holds Moshe is relating to their stature.

15 *Shemot* 24:1, 9.

as from Yitro[16] and from the daughters of Tzelofchad.[17] These stories show that Moshe was human. To be human is to not always know the answer and to sometimes learn the correct teaching from others. Therefore, why would Nadav and Avihu's giving rulings in front of their teacher be an obvious sin?

The second conjecture, that Nadav and Avihu chose not to have children, may initially seem to be pointing to something more straightforwardly wrong. After all, the first commandment given to mankind was to be fruitful and multiply.[18] What could be more obvious than that? After all, there is nothing as basic to the furtherance of society as procreation. But deeper thought reveals that this too is less obvious than it first appears, as the need for procreation is much more complicated on an individual level.

Though we often associate celibacy with other religious traditions, Judaism's verdict is more complicated than most people think. Not only was there a Talmudic sage who espoused it,[19] his position was accepted in the classical Jewish legal codes as a live option.[20] Moreover, ironically, if this was the sin of Nadav and Avihu, they would have been following Moshe rather than differing from him. Granted, Moshe had already had children before he separated from his wife, but that was before he grew in stature. According to the dominant understanding, once Moshe reached an elevated level of prophecy, he permanently separated from his wife.[21] Having been given this example of spiritual elevation, there certainly would have been room for Nadav and Avihu to think that celibacy was an appropriate path for them as well.

We now see that both of these examples constitute sins much more plausible than the one indicated by a simple reading of the biblical text. Given that a strong case could be made for the permissibility of either teaching in front of

16 *Shemot* 18:13–26.

17 *Bemidbar* 27:1–11.

18 *Bereshit* 1:28.

19 *Yevamot* 63b.

20 *Mishneh Torah, Hilchot Ishut* 15:3; *Shulchan Aruch, Even haEzer* 1:4.

21 One could say Moshe's celibacy was not a result of his lofty stature but rather due to his need to always be available for prophecy, but that need not have been the only reason for it. In any case, had Nadav and Avihu actually missed this distinction, they would have done no worse than Miriam and Aharon. See *Bemidbar* 12:5–8; Nataf, *Redeeming Relevance in Numbers*, 76–78.

Moshe or celibacy, we could understand Nadav and Avihu making a mistake in these ways or in ones similar to them.

Text and Context

We are now ready to return to the context within which Nadav and Avihu's deaths appears.

The continuation of the story involves many family members. Moshe first instructs Aharon's *cousins* to pull out the bodies; then he instructs his *brother*, Aharon, and Aharon's remaining two *sons*, Elazar and Itamar, about the laws of mourning. He tells them they are not allowed to fully mourn, but puts them at ease by saying that their *brothers*, the entire house of Israel, will do so in their stead. Immediately afterward, God speaks to Aharon about the issue of wine we mentioned earlier, explicitly directing it to him and his *sons*. And as the verses continue, the relationship between Aharon and his sons is placed under the spotlight.

The above observation makes it easier to notice the peculiar introduction of the main characters as "the sons of Aharon, Nadav and Avihu." While not technically wrong, this phrasing is somewhat unusual – the default is to present the names first and then their relationship to any others, i.e., "Nadav and Avihu, the sons of Aharon." That this is not coincidental is reinforced twice in the verses that follow. First we read, "Mishael and Eltzafan, the sons of Uziel," and later, "Elazar and Itamar, the sons of Aharon."[22] This is a strong hint that the relationship between Nadav and Avihu and their father deviates from the standard father-son relationship.[23]

A key word puts everything else into a fascinating perspective – the description of their fire as "*zara*" (foreign).[24] In Modern Hebrew, *zara* means someone of a different nation, but the Torah does not use the word in this way even once. Rather, *zara* almost always describes someone who is not of

22 *Vayikra* 10:4, 16.
23 See *Sifra, Acharei Mot* 1:1.
24 The feminine form of the word *zar*. Given that the word is generally used to describe men in the Torah, it is mostly found in the masculine form.

the *family*.[25] It is generally used to describe a non-priest, i.e., not of Aharon's family; and the word retains this connotation in the context of levirate marriage, specifically to describe an individual who is not the brother of a man who died childless.[26]

The Torah makes a point of describing the sin Nadav and Avihu committed with a word usually meaning "not of the family" – all the more so in this context of otherwise well-ordered family ties. It is no coincidence, then, that if we were to distill our emerging reading of the sin of Nadav and Avihu to its core, we would say that Aharon's two sons became foreign to their family; that is, they made themselves not their father's sons.

Amid all the other relatives involved in the greater episode of Nadav and Avihu's deaths, Aharon's younger children are quite clearly inserted into the story, taking the role previously held by their older brothers. Although Aharon dies almost forty years later, it already becomes clear at this point that his third son, Elazar, will take on his mantle – literally as well as figuratively – upon Aharon's death. The contrast is palpable. If the Torah is indicating that Nadav and Avihu had a problematic relationship with their father, there can be no more fitting sequel than showing that such would not be the case with Aharon's two younger sons.

In this context, we can better appreciate a strange narrative that unfolds after the death of Nadav and Avihu: Moshe objects to Aharon and his sons' refraining from eating from the sin offering due to their state of mourning. However, he curiously directs his ire at only the two remaining sons. Equally curious is the fact that it is not the sons who respond to Moshe but their father.

Based on what we have learned in this section, this makes perfect sense. Moshe is trying to see whether these sons are also estranged enough from Aharon to assert the authority he has given them when he addresses them instead of their father. On this score, they pass the test beautifully, remaining silent and allowing their father to speak for them.[27] With this, the traditional

25 The word is also used in a very similar way in the warning not to bring foreign incense on the altar (*Shemot* 30:9). It could be argued that here too, *zara* is primarily relating to something that does not belong in – i.e., is not of – the inner sanctum.

26 *Devarim* 25:5.

27 See *Yalkut Shimoni* 785:40 and Rashi on *Vayikra* 10:19, both of whom understand

lines of authority and hierarchy disrupted by the challenge of Nadav and Avihu are immediately restored.

Moreover, what we have described may well be the exact summary presented later on in an otherwise difficult verse. In enumerating Aharon's descendants the Torah doesn't stop at presenting who died and who survived, it presents the information in a highly stylized fashion, as follows: "And Nadav and Avihu died in front of God in their bringing a foreign fire in front of God . . . and Elazar and Itamar ministered (as priests) before Aharon their father."[28] The plain meaning of the verse is that the younger sons ministered on a continual basis, whereas the older sons had ministered only for a very short time. Yet telling us that Elazar and Itamar served *before their father* seems extraneous – except for the contrast it creates between them and their older brothers. The Torah wants us to see here that these sons served in front of their father – meaning under his tutelage – whereas the elder sons did not.

Some of the rabbis keenly pick up on the theme of Nadav and Avihu's detachment from the previous generation as well. The Talmud, for example, has the two walking behind their father and uncle saying, "When will these two die so that we can lead the generation?"[29] This is also what likely underlies one of the *midrashim* encountered earlier, that they gave a ruling in front of Moshe – who was not only the leader of the people but also their elder and uncle.

The upshot is that the events that took place after the sin of Nadav and Avihu elucidate the real issue behind whatever sin or sins they actually committed: They challenged the traditional hierarchy of children following their parents and juniors following their seniors. It is presumably this issue more than any individual sin that the Torah wants to bring to our attention.

Elazar and Itamar's silence as an act of deference to their father.

28 *Bemidbar* 3:4. While beyond the scope of this chapter, the contrast between the younger sons' service before *(al pnei)* their father and the older sons' service in front *(lifnei)* of God presents an interesting nuance to the tragedy of Nadav and Avihu.

29 *Sanhedrin* 52a.

How Could They?

Above, we said that many commentators sought to find a sin that Nadav and Avihu committed which would be more consonant with the elevated stature the Torah indicates they possessed. Yet even the more refined sins suggested are still somewhat surprising. Now that we have a better understanding of the Torah's broader message about Nadav and Avihu's disaffection with generational hierarchy and inability to serve "before their father," we are in a much better position to appreciate both their greatness and their sin.

While the Torah's indication of Nadav and Avihu's greatness puts them in the same league as Moshe and Aharon, the Midrash says they were actually greater.[30] Given what we have said about their insubordination, this is not surprising. As if Nadav and Avihu were actually greater than Moshe, we have an even stronger basis to understand why they would not have deferred to him when a question was asked of them. Perhaps Nadav and Avihu's greatness meant that they were able to both remember the Torah and work out its various teachings and implications better than Moshe.[31] Moshe would then have nothing to add. Indeed, they would have seen Moshe's objections to any of their behavior as the result of his weaker comprehension. Thus if Nadav and Avihu did serve while inebriated, for example, they could well have thought that they were adding a new dimension to the Divine service that Moshe could not comprehend. Likewise concerning the rest of the possible sins other commentators have conjectured, the central issue with all of them remains their predilection to ignore Moshe, precisely because of their greatness.

At this point, we may understand Nadav and Avihu's reluctance to follow Moshe and Aharon so well that we have a hard time seeing anything wrong with their behavior. Yet the Torah indicates that they erred. This tells us that younger people who are greater than their elders must still sometimes listen to them.

* * *

30 *Vayikra Rabba* 12:2.
31 The Talmud (*Menachot* 29b) presents this tension when Moshe is transported to the classroom of Rabbi Akiva and sees that the latter understands the Torah's implications better than he.

Young people are often in a hurry, impatient with conducting preliminary tests designed to ascertain that taking a rocket farther into space will not result in its destruction; or eager to dispense with yet another trial for an anti-cancer drug. "Let's go for it *now*, since according to my knowledge, there should be no problem," says the young man. The old man responds, "I remember Nadav and Avihu saying the same thing, and they were the finest minds the Jewish people ever saw – you know they were even greater than Moshe – and it didn't quite go as they planned."

One of the main things gained from experience is a better appreciation of how counterproductive it is to take things to the limit, without first testing the waters over and over again. This is not to say that risks always lead to a disaster; most of the time they don't. This is precisely why the young man is willing to go full steam ahead. For he who hasn't seen the likes of a Nadav and Avihu, the risks are only theoretical. But for the old man who has seen the devastating catastrophes that can result from lack of caution, the dangers are soberingly real. Thus, the rabbis teach that one should respect even a foolish old man, justifying their position by saying that his experience alone is worthy of respect.[32]

This can also help us understand another seemingly strange statement of the sages, that it is better to destroy when suggested by the elders than to build when suggested by the youth, for the former is true building and the latter actually destruction.[33] It is not necessarily that the older people know more; indeed, what is frustrating to young people is that their elders often know less. As they grow up and discover they possess more knowledge in certain areas, it is natural for them to be impatient with their parents' wisdom – a wisdom which often only appears to them as mere old-fashioned notions and knee-jerk reactions. Though the young are sometimes right, other times they realize too late that the caution of the elders is a healthy check to the impetuousness of youth.

The story of Nadav and Avihu serves as a paradigm for the need to factor in the experience of elders and to accept their leadership, even when there are younger people with greater raw intelligence and skill. For while the sons of

32 *Kiddushin* 33a.
33 *Nedarim* 40a.

Aharon may have been greater in terms of the wisdom that comes from knowledge, they were lacking the sagacity that comes from experience.

In its most vivid terms, the story of Aharon's sons shows us that one who ignores his elders is not equipped to live long enough to become a member of what he sees to be a superfluous generation. Even if he lives on, he will likely do so in intergenerational isolation. As he ignored his elders, so will his children ignore him – to the detriment of both generations, and to mankind, as well.

CHAPTER 5

The Blasphemer, the Egyptian and the Tribe of Dan

M ORE THAN ANY book of the Torah, *Vayikra* is a book of laws. Of the five books, it is the one with the most commandments. Given that it is also the shortest, this does not leave much room for stories. It follows then, that any story found in *Vayikra* should bring up certain questions: How does it fit in to the rest of the book? Is it qualitatively different from stories that appear elsewhere in the Torah?

This chapter will explore the episode of the "Israelite woman's son," who in the context of a nebulous altercation blasphemes and is sentenced to death (*Vayikra* 24:10–23). Not only does it elicit the above, *Vayikra*-specific questions, it would elicit its own questions no matter where it would be found.

The first thing we notice is the story's lack of detail. *Da'at Mikra* suggests that the missing information, such as why this man blasphemed for example, is not really important in terms of what the story is trying to tell us; that is why it is left out. But even if we are to follow this reasoning, we cannot fail to notice that the information that actually is presented is also highly stylized. For one, we learn only the blasphemer's mother's name and not that of his foreign father. But what stands out even more prominently is that the name of the blasphemer himself is not recorded. From these two items alone we get the sense that the Torah has a clear strategy with regard to what it omits and presents here, going well beyond its usually terse style.

For the main actor to be nameless while his mother is named is hard to miss. By the time we come to the end of this chapter, however, we will recognize that many of the particularities of this story reinforce the impression this naturally makes – that the Torah's main interest here is not about what the blasphemer did, but about something else entirely. Indeed, we will soon see additional indications that blasphemy is only secondary to the story.

Notably, several commentators get very involved in trying to understand the seemingly tangential question of whether this man needed to convert (it is tangential because Jewish tradition forbids blasphemy for gentiles as well[1]). These commentators intuit that what we really need to know about the blasphemer is his connection to his parents. To be more specific, the question they ultimately address is to what extent his foreign father impacted on what happened.

If we reflect on the story's context, it makes a great deal of sense that it is more about lineage than blasphemy. After all, the discussion takes place in *Vayikra*, a book very particular about whom Kohanim may marry and the ensuing profanation of their seed when these laws are disregarded. As we have pointed out in several places, we will not be able to understand an isolated story in *Vayikra* without an awareness of the thematic backdrop created by the book as a whole. With this in mind, let us now explore the story.

Defining the Genre

Although the details of this story are sparse, there are thankfully other ways for us to decipher its meaning. One such way is to compare and contrast it with other, similar stories in the Torah. There are only a few, but they are enough to provide us with a coherent discussion. They are the war with Amalek,[2] the Shabbat violator,[3] and Zimri and Kozbi.[4]

One of the defining features of this group of stories is that they seem to literally come out of nowhere. This is most pronounced in our story, wherein

1   See, for example, Ramban on *Vayikra* 24:10.
2   *Shemot* 17:8–16.
3   *Bemidbar* 15:32–36.
4   *Bemidbar* 25:1–15.

the Torah simply tells us that the antagonist "went out," providing no information with regard to where he came from.[5] This compares linguistically with Amalek's sudden approach. More fundamentally, however, none of the stories in this group has any obvious connection to what comes before or after it in the text.

A second defining characteristic of the genre is the rapid-fire presentation of the story, followed by an after-story. This characteristic is most pronounced in the story of the Shabbat violator, which is the one most similar to ours. (In fact, it is so similar that the two are often confused with one another.) That story is found much later – tucked away in the book of *Bemidbar*. Like our blasphemer, the Shabbat violator is brought to Moshe to decide what to do with him, which Moshe apparently doesn't know. In both stories, the transgressor is placed in some sort of jail called a *mishmar*. After that, God reveals the law and they are executed.[6] And if these parallels were not enough, the rabbis suggest that the two stories happened at the same time.[7]

Alongside the stories of the blasphemer, Amalek and the Shabbat transgressor, there is yet a fourth story in the genre we are exploring. This is the story of Zimri, the prince of Shimon, and Kozbi, the Midianite princess, who are summarily executed for trying to lead the Jewish people astray. The story follows the general pattern of the other three, while containing some unique parallels to the narrative of the blasphemer.

In the story of Zimri and Kozbi, we are told the name of the Jewish antagonist and his tribal affiliation only after the fact, just as we are told the name of the blasphemer's mother after the fact. More important, each is introduced in general terms, revealing only the character's nationality. In fact, the unusual term, *ish Yisrael* (an Israelite man), used to describe Zimri three times,[8] par-

5   *Vayikra* 24:10. Although several commentators on this verse, such as Ibn Ezra and Rabbenu Bachya, suggest the phrase means merely that the individual set out upon the field of action, the use of specifically this phrase in similar situations seems to imply more than that.

6   See *Torah Temima* on *Bemidbar* 15, note 103, which mentions some of the more subtle differences between the two narratives.

7   *Sifra, parashat Emor*, Section 14:5, which Rashi cites on *Vayikra* 24:12, makes the claim that they happened at the same time.

8   Twice in *Bemidbar* 25:8 and once in 25:14.

allels the initial description of the blasphemer's mother, Shlomit bat Divri, as *isha Yisraelit* (an Israelite woman).[9] The linguistic parallel only reinforces the narrative parallel: Zimri and Shlomit bat Divri are described as Israelites to emphasize that their partners are notably not.

Let us now turn to the differences between the story of the blasphemer in the book of *Vayikra* and the narrative of Zimri in *Bemidbar*, for when we analyze similar stories, the most important messages are often in the differences and not in the similarities.[10]

Anonymous Foreigners and Danite Intermarriages

Not only are the names of the main players[11] in both our story and that of Zimri and Kozbi given after the main narrative ends, when they are given we are presented their full names, going back all the way to their tribal elders. Yet there is also a highly significant difference between the two stories: Whereas in the latter story the names of both the man and the woman are mentioned, we learn only the name of the mother and not the father in the story of the blasphemer.[12] Rather than giving us the father's name, all we are told is that he is an Egyptian.

It is true that the Torah skips over the names of many of its relatively minor characters,[13] but when it does skip over names, it rarely discriminates within

9 *Vayikra* 24:10.

10 See Robert Alter, *The Art of Biblical Narrative* (New York: Basic Books, 1981), 47–59.

11 While we might have thought the blasphemer to be the main character in our story, the Torah tells it in such a way that even if he is the one to receive the actual sentence, it is his parents who are at the center of the narrative.

12 We cannot suggest that the father was not mentioned because he was a foreigner, as Kozbi was also a foreigner. However, there is an important difference between the stories which might answer this riddle: In the story of Zimri and Kozbi in the book of *Bemidbar*, the man and the woman themselves are the perpetrators of the sin. In our story here in *Vayikra*, the Torah concerns itself with the sinner's *parents*. Nevertheless, the fact that the Torah names both Zimri and Kozbi in their story creates the expectation that both parents' names in our story will be mentioned.

13 See Francis Nataf, "Shemot's Missing Names," *Jewish Bible Quarterly* 45:3 (July–September 2017), 193.

a group of characters of equal weight. Hence the lack of parallelism in the blasphemer's story is rare to begin with. This is reinforced by the equality of naming both players that is to be found in the story of Zimri and Kozbi, which forces us to conclude that the Torah is trying to get our attention. Less obvious, however, is why.

One famous midrash takes the following approach: that the father of the blasphemer was none other than the Egyptian taskmaster slain by Moshe.[14] In other words, he was a *specific* Egyptian, so evil that the Torah wanted to "erase his name."[15] Yet if such a key figure was literally the father of the blasphemer, one would have nonetheless expected the Torah to reveal his identity, if not his name.[16]

Whether we take the above midrash literally or not, the fact that his name is withheld while his nationality is revealed functions as an important literary device: it takes the focus away from the individual father and places it on the group to which he belongs. By doing so, the Torah deflects his paternal responsibility for the curser's sin onto the Egyptian nation as a whole.

The above point could even be strengthened if the father turned out to be the Egyptian taskmaster; it would be quite natural for us to blame that father, expecting such an evil man's son to be evil as well. Knowing this, the Torah prefers to hide the father's identity as much as possible in order to indicate that the real focus is not on the father but on his nation. Accordingly, *Bechor*

---

14 *Vayikra Rabba* 32:4. According to our understanding, the authors of the midrash saw the default here to be mentioning his name. Thus, identifying him as the Egyptian taskmaster explains why his name does not appear. Rabbi Akiva's opinion (*Shabbat* 96b) that the Shabbat violator was Tzelofchad seems to be coming from a similar angle. Hence we see that mentioning names is considered the general default in these stories.

15 See *Chizkuni* on *Vayikra* 24:10–11, who finds support for this identification from a particularly insightful – if somewhat speculative – angle: That the reason the blasphemer cursed God's Name is because he had just found out that Moshe killed his father with it (as is traditionally understood by many of the rabbis; see *Shemot Rabba* 1:29).

16 Though we do not reject such a possibility outright, the default remains that the man in question was a random Egyptian who married Shlomit and quite possibly was still living and present with her in the wilderness at this time. When not otherwise indicated, this will be our assumption throughout the chapter.

Shor reminds us of Pharoah's initial proclamation about the Jewish God's ir-relevance[17] and the resulting likelihood of disrespect toward that God by the entire nation. With this in mind, our story could be read as a warning that the Egyptians do not belong with the Jews, and this difficult incident as the outcome of not heeding that warning.

Yet there might be an even larger issue here. By indicating the father was an Egyptian, the Torah could be drawing our attention not to his personal heritage but to the fact that he was more generally not a native-born Jew. In other words, the issue is that of bringing *any* gentiles into the Jewish people. True, the Torah clearly allows for converts (and it goes out of its way to call for their proper treatment). In fact, I have argued elsewhere that the Torah iden-tifies an out-and-out need for them.[18] But the Torah also expresses concern with regard to taking in converts indiscriminately. Part of the Jewish trajec-tory is protracted refinement over many generations. Though individuals can be assimilated into this process, the chance of successfully assimilating large groups of foreigners who have not participated in this slow historical process is quite slim.

It is much easier to accept no gentiles than to be selective about which ones are accepted. And since the smallness of the Jewish nation has often been a concern, the temptation of the Jewish nation to expand its historically small numbers by attracting converts wholesale has surfaced at more than one juncture in history. In light of both the problem of mass conversion and the temptation to employ it, the Torah wanted to jolt the Jewish nation into understanding its possible consequences. Moreover, it is now at this crucial juncture, before the Jews were to enter their land and be in a situation where they could attract large number of converts, that this teaching would be most appropriate. Thus it is quite reasonable to suggest that the impact created by the sin of blasphemy and the sinner's unusual public execution could well be the mechanism through which the Torah sought to impress this message upon the Jews.

The negative impact of improper converts is clearly an important aspect of

17 *Bechor Shor, Da'at Zekenim* on *Vayikra* 24:10, with reference to *Shemot* 5:2.
18 Francis Nataf, *Redeeming Relevance Numbers*, 134–139.

what the Torah wants us to understand here, but it is not the whole story. As we shall see, the Torah does not appear to be placing all of the blame on the father. Except for obvious cases where one parent is clearly the perpetrator, this makes sense; as we should normally assume that some blame should be assigned to each parent (it being understood that final *responsibility* for the act belongs to the child alone). In fact, as some commentators point out, it can be argued that it is usually the mother who has the greater influence on the child.[19]

If Egyptian nationality was the problem on the blasphemer's paternal side, what was the problem on his maternal side? Given that we do not have much more to go on, some commentaries identify the mother's "defect" as her tribal affiliation – she was of the tribe of Dan.[20] These commentators generally follow a Talmudic statement that views this tribe as being overly quick to seek litigation,[21] based on the blessing given to Dan by Ya'akov.[22] And so when this Danite mother's son lost a case, it brought him to blasphemy. However, the problem with the mother's tribal identity may actually come from elsewhere.

If intermarriage is the problem, here is a good place to point out that it takes two to tango. And the fact that the mother, Shlomit, is from Dan may actually go a long way in explaining her willingness to be involved in such a marriage. Indeed, it is likely not a coincidence that intermarriage is the Achilles heel of Dan's most famous descendant, Shimshon.

Dan is the rearguard of the Jewish nation.[23] Consequently, he is more exposed to foreigners than most of the other tribes. As opposed to the vanguard (Yehuda), who is equally exposed, the rearguard is likely to encounter more

---

19 See Rabbenu Bachya on *Vayikra* 24:11. This point would be strengthened by a literal reading of the earlier midrash that the blasphemer's father was the Egyptian taskmaster, since in that case the child would never have known him.

20 *Chizkuni, Da'at Zekenim* on *Vayikra* 24:11. Given that a character's tribal affiliation is not always mentioned with his or her name, it is reasonable to say that its mention is purposeful. Moreover, the midrash in *Vayikra Rabba* 32:5 also sees the mother's unusual name as an expression of her culpability. But see also Abarbanel on the same verse, who has a positive interpretation of her name.

21 *Pesachim* 4a.

22 *Bereshit* 49:16: "Dan will judge his nation."

23 *Bereshit* 49:17.

surreptitious attempts to attack the Jewish people. Powerful enemies will openly attack from the front, but attacking the rear is a tactic generally[24] taken by those who must find alternative ways of bringing an enemy down. Hence Dan is a tribe likely to encounter those who, for example, pretend to be allies in order to camouflage their actual hostility. In the case of the Israelites, this would include enemy women seeking marriages with Jewish men for ulterior motives. This is the exact scenario of the story of Shimshon.[25]

But even more revealing than the story of Shimshon is another, less well-known one. Toward the end of the book of *Shofetim* is found one of the Bible's strangest narratives, usually referred to as the Idol of Micha.[26] Micha is a rather murky figure who decides to set up an idolatrous altar in the middle of a Jewish habitation. Meanwhile, on a journey to conquer a new enclave for their settlement, a Danite war party comes upon the altar and steals it, subsequently setting it up in their newly conquered city in the northernmost section of the Land of Israel.[27] While Dan is not the only tribe that shows itself lacking during this difficult period in Jewish history, its behavior seems markedly non-Israelite. Moreover, it is the only tribe to be given one inheritance only to subsequently seek another one – significantly, at the very end of the Jewish settlement. How are we to understand all of this?

One notable hint is that the new Danite city is near Tzidon (Sidon).[28] This town, bearing the name of Canaan's oldest son,[29] is the home of one of the Bible's most famous villains, Izevel (Jezebel). Daughter of the king of Tzidon, she marries King Achav of the northern kingdom of Israel, bringing idolatry and a level of ruthless immorality of which even her evil husband is not capable. By the seemingly casual mention of Tzidon in the story of the Danite

---

24 The most famous counterexample of a nation that has the power for a frontal attack but attacks from the rear out of plain malice is Amalek. See Nataf, *Redeeming Relevance in Deuteronomy*, 86–87.

25 *Shofetim* 13–16.

26 *Shofetim* 17–18.

27 Whether it was part of the original borders that the Jews were given a Divine mandate to conquer is a point of contention. See R. Yigal Ariel, *Oz ve'Anava* (Chispin, Israel: Midreshet haGolan, 1995), 346–347.

28 *Shofetim* 18:28.

29 *Bereshit* 10:15.

move north, the text is revealing the tribe's state of mind. As with Achav later on, Dan too might have been interested in advancing Israelite settlement with the help of foreigners more technologically and commercially advanced – even if it came at the cost of highly corrosive moral influences.

Most important, however, is that Dan seeks the position of bridgehead at the northern end of the Jewish settlement even when it was not given to the tribe. Dan is *uniquely* motivated to find a territory in which it will be the conduit between the Jews and the gentiles.

Of course, there are contexts in which good can be gained specifically from some of the Jews' northern neighbors. For example, Hiram, king of neighboring Tzur (Tyre), helps King Shlomo build the Temple.[30] But this does not take away from the fact that interaction with foreigners is a risky venture that should only be pursued with a great deal of forethought. More specifically, *successful* interaction with foreigners involves both not overestimating its benefit and not underestimating its danger. If one's own lifestyle is not much more refined than that of the foreigners, the danger will be easily overlooked. That which we read about Dan being involved with idolatry in the process of its conquest is no coincidence. It is the book of *Shofetim's* way of hinting that the tribe's move closer to the gentiles was not just geographical but ideological as well.[31]

This brings us back to the curser's mother. If his father's mentality may have ultimately been the source of his behavior, it is his mother who seemingly allowed the mentality to seep into her son and, ultimately, into the Jewish people. Given what we have seen about the nature of her tribe, this should not surprise us. Long before the Danites' penchant for connection with gentiles would reach its climax in the days of Shimshon, the Torah warns them – and any others who might take a similar position – of the great dangers that such an approach toward gentiles entails.

---

30 Although even there, interaction with gentiles ultimately cost Shlomo more than half his kingdom (*I Melachim* 11:1–11).

31 See *Midrash Tanchuma, Ki Tissa* 13, which identifies Dan as the most inferior of the tribes. See also Francis Nataf, "Shimshon and the Gates of Chevron," *Torah Musings Journal* (May 26, 2014), https://www.torahmusings.com/2014/05/shimshon-and-the-gates-of-chevron/.

The Torah's Loneliest Story

Before we return to our final look at the whole group of stories to which that of the blasphemer belongs, there is one more aspect of this particular story we need to consider, and that is its placement toward the end of the book of *Vayikra*. This issue relates not only to the narrative; one should also wonder why the laws of blasphemy that follow it have been placed here as well. Would they not have more naturally found their place in the legal sections of *Shemot* or *Devarim*, where one generally finds these type of laws, or at the very least in the section of *Vayikra* where we find more general laws?

In fact, the placement of the laws of blasphemy may be exceptional for another reason – their attachment to a related story. This makes them one of only a few sets of laws that follow an illustrative episode. But when we look at another proximate example, also in the book of *Vayikra* – the legislation that priests not drink alcohol before performing the sacrificial service, right after the death of Aharon's sons[32] – we notice an important difference. That the story of the death of Aharon's sons and the subsequent laws of drunkenness is placed in the larger context of the inauguration of the Mishkan, makes narrative sense. It is part and parcel of that story. In contrast, the story of the blasphemer with *its* accompanying laws does not seem to be related to the entire, brief time frame in which the book of *Vayikra* takes place.

If stories that did not take place in *Vayikra*'s time frame were nevertheless needed for illustration, there should have been a wealth of them. But there are not – there is only this one.

The issue just raised can be addressed by going back to what we believe is the main message of the blasphemer story. We saw earlier that this message is the need to be very selective in accepting converts who will ultimately intermarry with the rest of the Jewish population. We also mentioned the importance of emphasizing this to the Israelites before it would become a practical issue when they entered the Land of Israel; hence, its discussion right before the section pertaining to the land's holiness.

---

32   See p. 82, where we lay out further evidence as to why the law is indeed coming as a response to what happened.

While we have already seen that the placement of the story of the blasphemer at the end of the book of *Vayikra* is significant, its placement in the highly non-narrative book of *Vayikra* altogether may be even more important: Blasphemy is not found very often among Jews in the Bible, and consequently the story would have been shocking anywhere.[33] But for it to come up specifically in the middle of the Torah's longest legal section is clearly *meant* to shock. Given the magnitude and severity of the danger, this is precisely what is called for. Indeed, there could not have been any better way to drive home the consequences of marrying inappropriate converts than to have such an outrageous story in the middle of a book that is all about holiness and separation.

Stories in the Blink of an Eye

The story of the blasphemer is part of a small group – or genre – of four stories possessing similar characteristics. They can be summarized as follows: There is a sudden, destabilizing threat that the Israelites were not immediately prepared to deal with. That lack of preparation – among other things – involves their inability to turn to Moshe, who in turn is unable to provide leadership and, consequently, requires the assistance of others. In the end, however, the threat is swiftly redressed and the Torah proceeds to tell us its consequences.

The action in these stories moves very quickly, giving us a palpable feel for what happened. The need to rush through them is one of the reasons why names are not given until after the end of the stories; names would just get in the way. Only once the crisis is over can we go back to such details. The sense of limited time reflects the need to act right away. As speed is of utmost importance, the Israelites and their leaders must resort to improvisation and alacrity in order to contain something that would otherwise inflict serious – perhaps even fatal – damage.

These four stories show emergencies. Extraordinary resources must be

---

33 See Rabbi S. D. Luzzatto (*Vayikra* 24:10) who intimates that what sets the law of blasphemy apart is that it was so inconceivable, it had to be accompanied by a story of it actually happening.

mobilized to control an otherwise dangerous situation. As we all know, not every emergency ends happily, and no matter how many contingencies we prepare for, emergencies will always be a part of life. Hence – as in all other parts of life – we are well advised to see what is said about them in the "Tree of Life."

The unusual content and presentation of these stories implies that while we may sometimes act too rashly, there are also times when rash action is the only way to prevent an even greater debacle. Precisely because the Torah espouses living an ideal, thought-out life of ethics and spirituality, it also needs to make sure we don't get carried away by our thought-world. It should already be clear enough from the Torah's interest in real life that there is a time for action as well as a time for thought. But that is not enough. What these stories drive home is that action sometimes needs to be immediate. In such situations there is no time for thinking through the "best" solution.

In some of these stories, Moshe was able to go to God to be told what to do. But that is only because his deputies immediately took control of the situation and quarantined the threat.[34] There is wisdom in what the deputies did. Some emergencies require people to act even before waiting for instructions from above. But there was also wisdom at the top. In these situations, leaders cannot stand on ceremony and worry about the fallout, either from their seeking help – both human and Divine – or from allowing others to take independent action.

In the end, the wisdom required for emergencies depends on the ability to discern between when we are facing an emergency and when we are not. For just as acting too slowly can be a problem when not required, so too can acting too quickly.

Indeed, the background in the rest of the book of *Vayikra* is about setting up a model society in a thought-out and orderly fashion. The ability to deal with emergencies is how we preserve such a society. But even more important is creating a society worth preserving. And as we have seen in our discussions in this volume, following the blueprint set up more generally in *Vayikra* may well be the key.

34 See *Ha'amek Davar* on *Vayikra* 24:12, who states that in the case of the blasphemer, the intention of locking up the accused included protecting him from the anger of the mob.